eat what you love
DIABETES COOKBOOK

eat what you love
DIABETES COOKBOOK

Comforting, Balanced Meals

Lori Zanini, RD, CDE

SONOMA
PRESS

TRADEMARKS: Sonoma Press and the Sonoma Press logo are trademarks or registered trademarks of Callisto Media Inc. and/or its affiliates, in the United States and other countries, and may not be used without written permission. All other trademarks are the property of their respective owners. Sonoma Press is not associated with any product or vendor mentioned in this book.

Front cover photography © Melina Hammer; back cover photography © Tanya Zouev/Stockfood, Keller & Keller Photography/Stockfood, and People Pictures/Stockfood

Interior photography © Tanya Zouev/Stockfood, p.2 & 187; Keller & Keller Photography/Stockfood, p.2 & 67; People Pictures/Stockfood, p.2 &159; Sara Remington/Stocksy, p.6; Amir Kaljikovic/Stocksy, p.11; Trinette Reed/Stocksy, p.12; Miquel Llonch/Stocksy, p.21; Kelly Cline/iStock, p.25; Ina Peters/Stocksy, p.27; Ina Peters/Stocksy, p.28; Harald Walker/Stocksy, p.35; Gräfe & Unzer Verlag/Hoersch, Julia/Stockfood, p.40; Davide Illini/Stocksy, p.49; Jonathan Gregson/Stockfood, p.54; Nadine Greeff/Stocksy, p.74; Martin Dyrlov/Stockfood, p.82; Yelena Strokin/Stockfood, p.91; PhotoCuisine/Thys/Supperdelux/Stockfood, p.96; Keller & Keller Photography/Stockfood, p.104; Keller & Keller Photography/Stockfood, p.113; Keller & Keller Photography/Stockfood, p.118; Simone Neufing/Stockfood, p.122; Gräfe & Unzer Verlag/Schardt, Wolfgang/Stockfood, p.129; Tanja Major/Stockfood, p.132; People Pictures/Stockfood, p.138; Westermann & Buroh Studios/Stockfood, p.147; George Crudo/Stockfood, p.152; Tatjana Ristanic/Stocksy, p.162; Westermann & Buroh Studios/Stockfood, p.169; aGräfe & Unzer Verlag/Rynio, Jörn/Stockfood, p.174; PhotoCuisine/Sirois, Alain/Stockfood, p.180; Keller & Keller Photography/Stockfood, p.192; Laura Adani/Stocksy, p.196

ISBN: Print 978-1-943451-44-9
eBook 978-1-943451-45-6

In loving memory of my aunt,
Dr. Dellmar Walker

Contents

Foreword

If you've been diagnosed with diabetes, or even prediabetes, you are *not* alone. Diabetes is the fastest-growing global condition today, affecting millions of people. There is no cure for diabetes, except for extreme cases where weight-loss surgery in morbidly obese patients has proven to reduce severe insulin resistance. Depending on the stage of the condition, however, diabetes can be controlled very well. In some early cases, it can even be reversed.

Since diabetes is environmental as much as it is genetic, modifying some causal factors can make a difference. Getting adequate sleep, sitting less, coping with stress differently, and substituting bad habits with good ones are a few examples of changes that can help manage diabetes.

Diet is another factor that plays a vital role. It's essential to remember that a diabetes diagnosis does not prohibit you from enjoying *most* food you eat on a daily basis. "Nothing is off limits" is important information that people with diabetes need to know. Some nonfood items should be reduced significantly for sure. Attending diabetes education classes will give you a better idea of the distinction between food and nonfood, which is very confusing these days. To be safe, check food labels for ingredients that read as difficult-to-pronounce chemicals—these should be considered nonfood items. While you can still enjoy most foods, knowledge of "how much is enough" plays a critical role when choosing food categories, types, and amounts to make up a balanced diet.

In addition to preparing your meals appropriately, consuming them in controlled portions in a timely manner will help maintain your metabolic rhythm. If you can also keep a regular activity routine, your diabetes will be managed much more consistently, together with other metabolic factors such as blood pressure and cholesterol. Keeping all these factors controlled is an important part of preventing possible complications including, but not limited to, stroke, heart attack, and kidney and liver diseases.

As an endocrinologist, my goal is to help my patients avoid or prevent serious complications from diabetes. Lifestyle modifications are fundamental in managing metabolic conditions and have the highest impact on a person's health and well-being. I've had the privilege of working with Lori Zanini as one of the certified diabetes educators we physicians heavily rely on to provide patients and families with these valuable pieces of information and tireless guidance. Lori's expertise as a registered dietitian added tremendously to her contribution in this role.

In this book, Lori has compiled simple recipes and snack ideas, always paired with a breakdown of nutritional values that will help guide you in creating safe yet delicious dishes. I hope everyone can enjoy their favorite foods while continuing to pursue their endeavor to be healthy, and I believe this book is a valuable resource for achieving that goal.

—*Nandar Swe, MD*

Introduction

If you have ever felt overwhelmed by your diabetes diagnosis and unsure about what to eat, you are not alone. Every year 1.7 million Americans are diagnosed with diabetes, yet many of them do not receive the vital nutrition education that could actually improve their blood sugar levels, prevent diabetes complications, and increase their energy to strengthen their overall quality of life. Diabetes is a condition that is largely self-managed. This means that the positive habits you practice on a daily basis have the potential to improve the outcome of your health. You can even begin noticing an improvement in your diabetes and blood sugar levels after eating just a single healthy, balanced meal . . . now that's motivating!

If you are like most people, the subject of food—what you are (or aren't) eating, and how to eat properly—is a daily topic of conversation. Despite the constant buzz of new diet trends, celebrity diets, and detoxes, I encourage you to realize that nutrition is a science, not an opinion, so you need to get your facts from trusted health professionals. Even though we have more nutrition information at our fingertips than ever before, it can be challenging to recognize a dieting fad versus a real, sustainable way of eating that will actually benefit our bodies. And is it too much to ask that we actually *enjoy* the food we are eating? Not at all. The good news is that eating healthy with diabetes can be enjoyable, satisfying, and delicious!

As a registered dietitian and certified diabetes educator, I have worked with individuals at all stages of their diabetes journeys. Despite the length of time someone has lived with diabetes, their first question to me is always the same: "Can I still eat (insert favorite food)?" The answer is always yes! Everyone has a favorite food they just aren't willing to give up, and when it comes to managing your blood sugar, we don't need to eliminate foods that seem off-limits. The key is focusing on the amount we eat, how often, and when we eat it.

Growing up in the South, I learned that food should be enjoyed and shared with those you love. My Tennessee roots made a lasting impression on me, giving me an appreciation for home cooking, family meals, and traditional comfort foods, and today I have successfully incorporated these traditions and their principles into my professional practice. Meanwhile, my holistic approach has helped thousands of individuals improve their blood sugar, diabetes, and overall health. I have found that the meals we decide to eat are never *just* about the food. Perhaps just as important are the people eating with you, the time you put into preparing the food, and even the emotions the food can elicit. Knowing this, I work with my clients to achieve balance and satisfaction in the meal plans we create.

We know short-term diets don't work, but when we incorporate our favorite foods, they become sustainable, lifelong plans that will help us thrive for years to come.

We know that short-term diets don't work, but when we incorporate our favorite foods, they become sustainable, lifelong plans that will help us thrive for years to come. In my experience, I have found that when we focus on the positive benefits of the foods we eat, we start to appreciate food for the health it can bring to our bodies, rather than feeling deprived for any foods omitted. No one should think a diabetes diagnosis requires eating meals different from those of your family and friends. The truth is, a diabetes meal plan is simply a healthy, balanced way of eating, one from which we can all benefit. Since carbohydrates are the main source of energy for our bodies, completely eliminating carbs is (thankfully) not the answer either. Research has proven that eating consistent quantities of quality carbohydrates throughout the day, combined with balanced meals, is the best way to stabilize blood sugar and lose weight.

This book will educate you on how food affects your blood sugar, while empowering you to make the best decisions for your personal preferences. By taking the mystery out of healthy eating, and debunking all the inaccurate nutrition trends the media likes to promote, I will give you the tools to be more in control of your food choices. You will then learn how to use real, whole foods to create simple and delicious meals you will find yourself making over and over again.

I invite you now to come inside my kitchen and see how I have helped thousands of individuals control their blood sugar and manage their diabetes—all while truly enjoying their mealtimes and eating what they love!

Food and Diabetes

With more than 29 million Americans living with diabetes, this condition is growing faster than ever. After a diabetes diagnosis, choosing what to eat can often seem daunting, but it is completely normal to feel confused about how food will impact your blood sugar. The good news is that once you understand how food is utilized by your body, choosing the best types of foods in the right portion sizes will become much easier. You will be empowered to learn that there's a lot you can do yourself to manage and control your diabetes. Before you know it, eating healthy will turn into a routine. I have had many clients tell me that their diabetes diagnosis was the motivation they needed to improve their habits, and now they feel better and more in control of their health than ever before!

What Diabetes Means for Your Diet

When we talk about food and diabetes, there are several key items you need to understand. The timing of your meals, portion sizes, and the actual foods you eat are the most important factors in controlling your blood sugar.

TIMING OF MEALS

Too many people tell me that after receiving their diabetes diagnosis they started skipping entire meals in the hopes that this strategy would improve their blood sugar. The fact is, this habit will work against you and could lower your metabolic rate, which would actually make it more challenging to lose weight—not less. It's important to realize that there are several organs at work managing blood sugar throughout the day. The pancreas secretes the hormone insulin, which is released after eating. Insulin in turn helps the sugars broken down from carbohydrates enter the cells to be used for energy. Additionally, the liver stores a form of sugar called glycogen. The purpose of the liver glycogen is to maintain blood sugar levels during periods of fasting. If we do not eat balanced meals throughout the day at regular times, or if we go too long without eating, the liver may think we are fasting, and we want to prevent this from happening. An additional consideration is that if you are taking diabetes medications, skipping meals could possibly cause hypoglycemia, or low blood sugar, which we also want to avoid.

To prevent blood sugar from rising, I recommend eating within 1 hour of waking up. After your first meal of the day, you should eat at least every 4 to 5 hours. Then, make sure you don't go more than 10 hours overnight without eating. For example, if you eat dinner at 8 p.m., you should consume your breakfast by 6 a.m. This simple tip will not only help stabilize your blood sugar levels but also increase your metabolism and promote more appropriate portion sizes at your meals. This is because when we eat smaller, balanced meals throughout the day, we are more in tune with our hunger levels. This mealtime consistency will help regulate your blood sugar and energy, and improve your diabetes control.

CARBOHYDRATES

Macronutrients are essential nutrients that provide the calories our bodies require to operate properly. These macronutrients consist of carbohydrates, protein, and fat, all of which work together to provide the energy our bodies need to help run essentially every function. Carbohydrates, or carbs, are the main source of energy, so eliminating them entirely is not a realistic solution for controlling diabetes; in fact, the consumption of nutrient-dense carbohydrates is vital to achieving good health and blood sugar control. However, it's extremely important to choose the healthiest types of carbs. Many people are surprised to learn that carbs are found in all fruits, dairy products, and whole grains—even some starchy vegetables are high in carbs, such as sweet potatoes, corn, winter squash, and green peas. I encourage individuals to choose carbs that are high in fiber. The higher a food's fiber content, the slower the body will digest it, and the less likely it will be to cause a spike in blood sugar. Consuming consistent quantities of carbohydrates at each meal helps the pancreas know how much insulin to secrete, and makes the body better able to respond.

SERVING SIZES

The best technique for ensuring that we consume the appropriate quantity of carbohydrates at each meal is simply by counting them. This information can be found on the nutrition facts label on packages. Generally, it is recommended that an individual eat 30 to 60 grams of carbohydrates per meal. Women trying to lose weight may wish to aim closer to 30 grams of carbohydrates per meal, while men trying to lose weight may wish to aim closer to 45 grams. If you have any special concerns, always reach out to your health care provider or seek the help of a personal registered dietitian or certified diabetes educator, who can help customize additional guidance as needed.

If this daily monitoring sounds daunting, don't be intimidated: This book gives you the tools that make it easy to stay on track. All recipes in the following chapters are accompanied by a complete breakdown of nutritional information, with the total number of carbohydrates clearly called out in the panel. Simply mix and match mains and sides to assemble any number of delectable balanced meals.

FOOD LABELS

It's always helpful to check food labels when they are available. The most important figure you need to locate is the total carbohydrates number, which currently includes sugar and fiber. To find out how many carbohydrates are in a packaged food, simply look at the serving size and then the total carbohydrates. The number of total carbohydrates includes both the sugars and fiber found in the food.

Remember, women trying to lose weight should aim for approximately 30 grams of total carbohydrates per meal, and men trying to lose weight should aim for approximately 45 grams of total carbohydrates per meal.

In 2018, the FDA will also start showing how much added sugar is contained in specific foods. This will be very helpful because these added sugars lack fiber, digest quickly, and get into our blood rapidly, so reducing these sugars is important. Look out for words like syrup, honey, sugar, molasses, sucrose, and lactose in the ingredients list. If you see any of these words, it indicates that the manufacturer has added these types of supplementary sugars to their product.

The Power of Meal Planning

When we think in advance about what we are going to eat, we almost always make better choices. Once we're hungry, we tend to choose foods that are less healthy, to eat faster, and to consume larger portions. Taking the time to plan what you are going to eat throughout the week ahead will make an incredible difference in your diabetes management.

Ensuring that you plan for the foods you enjoy most, including your favorite comfort foods, will help empower you to create sustainable habits that will improve your health for years to come. Remember, you can still eat those seemingly forbidden foods you love, whether it's chicken pot pie, meatloaf, French fries, pasta salad, or chocolate chip cookies; the trick is understanding portion control, learning how to make improvements in nutrition while cooking, and creating balanced meals.

PLANNING FOR THE WEEK AHEAD

When you start to think about what you will eat throughout the week, bear in mind the following important considerations:

1. **Think about your schedule for the week.** Will there be any meals you will eat outside your home? This could include lunch meetings, birthday parties, happy hours, celebration dinners, or any other events. Also consider if there are any days you might be busier than normal and more likely to order fast food or pick up food to go. Assessing your schedule will provide you with the necessary information to determine how much food you will need and which meals you will need to plan. While it's not necessary to eat all your meals at home or be any less social than others, having a plan can help you set yourself up for success. Once you have evaluated your schedule, make plans to improve where possible. Could you bring your own food for that lunch meeting? For the dinner celebration, can you choose a restaurant that you know offers some great options for you? What if you plan to bring a snack or prepare your meal ahead of time on those extra-busy days? There are many solutions, but finding the ones that best fit your needs, schedule, and food preferences should be your number one priority.

2. **Evaluate your pantry.** Each week, take an inventory of the foods you already have in your kitchen. Use this as a starting point to plan your meals and to inspire what you will eat that week. This will not only help reduce your grocery bill and eliminate food waste, but also give you a better sense of how much you're eating on a weekly basis.

3. **Plan your meals.** Decide which meals you would like to eat throughout the week. An important aspect of planning your meals is to ensure these are meals you actually enjoy and will look forward to eating. Taking this simple step will help prevent cravings and promote better adherence to your meal plan, because including meals you truly take pleasure in will ensure you won't feel deprived but rather in control of both your food intake and blood sugar.

FOOD PREP

Next, it's time to put your plan into action. Designate Sunday as your day to prepare food for the upcoming week—this way you won't have to think about food prep on busy workdays, and you'll start the week off right. Advance prep might include washing and chopping vegetables, portioning out snacks in small containers, or even going ahead and cooking specific dishes to reheat for lunch and dinner. This is an opportunity to do anything that will save you time in the kitchen throughout the week and make you more likely to eat the meals you have planned.

SNACKS

One of the best reasons to eat a snack is to prevent yourself from being overly hungry when you arrive at your next meal. This will prepare you to eat the most appropriate types of food, while keeping your portion sizes in check.

Go-To Snacks

Create your own snack by pairing a food from the left column (carb) with a food from the right column (protein):

FOODS WITH 15 GRAMS OF CARBOHYDRATES	FOODS WITH PROTEIN
1 cup berries	½ cup cottage cheese
1 organic corn tortilla	1 hardboiled egg or 2 egg whites
2 slices crispbread	6 ounces plain Greek yogurt
1 small whole fruit (apple, pear, orange, etc.)	1 to 2 tablespoons natural nut butter
½ cup cooked oatmeal	1 to 2 ounces salmon or tuna
3 cups air-popped popcorn	1 string cheese
½ cup cooked quinoa	1 to 2 ounces organic tofu
½ small sweet potato	1 to 2 ounces turkey or chicken
1 slice 100% whole-wheat bread	¼ cup unsalted nuts
½ whole-wheat pita bread	

If it has been less than 4 or 5 hours since your last meal, it is best to choose snacks that are not high in carbohydrates: Focus on nonstarchy vegetables, small amounts of healthy fats, and protein. Here are some examples:

- 1 to 2 cups nonstarchy raw vegetables such as bell peppers, cucumbers, tomatoes, or leafy greens
- ¼ cup unsalted nuts
- 6 ounces plain Greek yogurt with cinnamon
- 1 string cheese

If it has been more than 4 or 5 hours since your last meal, it is important to include one serving of carbohydrates (15 grams of carbs) in addition to a protein source. For example:

- 1 cup blueberries with ¼ cup cottage cheese
- 1 ounce natural cheese with whole-wheat crackers
- 1 tablespoon natural almond butter on 1 slice 100% whole-wheat bread
- 1 hardboiled egg with a small whole fruit such as an apple or pear

The Balanced Plate

With the meal planning and preparation completed, the final step is to create your balanced meals. Learning how to serve yourself the variety of food your body needs may seem like a simple concept, but you first have to learn which foods fall into each category. Once you understand how to categorize the different foods, you will be able to plan and order all your meals with ease.

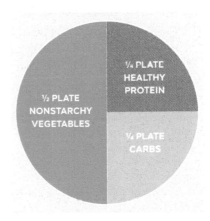

What does a balanced plate consist of for individuals with diabetes? It is recommended that half of your plate comes from nonstarchy vegetables, one-fourth from a healthy protein, and the other fourth from carbohydrates.

Let's take a look at which foods fall into each category:

Carbohydrates. See the portion sizes of commonly consumed foods that contain carbohydrates on page 21. Just remember that all fruit, starches, and liquid dairy products contain carbohydrates.

Healthy protein. It's important to include a healthy source of protein at every meal, since this does not raise blood sugar. On the contrary, protein actually helps stabilize our blood sugar and keeps us full longer than carbohydrates do. Examples of healthy protein sources include skinless chicken, pork tenderloin, turkey breast, fish, eggs, and natural cheese. Vegetarian sources of protein include beans, lentils, tofu, tempeh, seitan, and green peas. Be aware that while vegetarian protein sources are high in fiber and cholesterol-free, they do contain carbohydrates in addition to protein. Nuts and nut butters are also considered a source of protein, but they also contain (good) fats, so portions should be limited.

Nonstarchy vegetables. These types of vegetables are full of filling fiber, antioxidants, and plant compounds called phytochemicals that have been reported to prevent many chronic diseases. Including these as a regular part of your diet ensures your consumption of a variety of essential vitamins and nutrients. Examples of nonstarchy vegetables to eat at every meal include mushrooms, celery, green leafy vegetables, cucumbers, onions, radishes, beets, zucchini, tomatoes, bell peppers, chayote, squash, okra, cauliflower, broccoli, asparagus, eggplants, and artichokes.

For vegetables that contain starches, you will want to be aware of the portion sizes you are consuming. Starchy vegetables include corn, potatoes, peas, and winter squash (butternut, acorn, etc.).

TIPS FOR CREATING A BALANCED PLATE

Check the size of your plate. It's no surprise that the larger our plates, the more our portions tend to grow. Make sure that your dinner plates are no more than 9 inches across to help prevent the urge to fill your plate too full.

Use your measuring cups. I've had many individuals tell me they thought they were eating 1 cup of pasta, when it really ended up being 2 cups. Try to avoid "eyeballing" portion sizes when you are at home; instead, measure your portions in a measuring cup to ensure the amount of food you think you are eating is truly accurate. And the more you measure, the better you will get at "eyeballing"!

Look for color. You may have heard the expression "we eat with our eyes." This is true! The more appealing your plate looks, the more likely you will stick to your healthy eating habits. Bonus: The more colorful the produce you consume, the greater the variety of antioxidants from which you are benefitting!

Add flavor—don't take it away! It's a common myth that eating healthier meals means you will subsequently be eating less flavorful food. This isn't the case at all. I encourage you to get creative and *increase* flavor in your food. Some of my favorite flavorful additions are fresh herbs (cilantro, basil, thyme, mint, etc.), cinnamon, citrus juices (lemon, lime), jalapeño, ginger, and garlic.

Serving Sizes for Common Foods

Not all foods come with a food label. When we are away from home, it may be challenging to know how many carbohydrates are in the foods we are eating. With a little practice, however, you can count your carbohydrates in any eating situation. Here is a list of some common foods and the portion sizes that contain approximately 15 grams of carbohydrates:

- ½ small banana
- ½ cup cooked beans or lentils
- 1 cup berries
- ⅓ cup cooked brown rice
- 1 organic corn tortilla
- 1 small whole fruit (orange, apple, pear, etc.)
- ½ cup green peas
- 1 cup milk (nonfat, 2%, or whole)
- ½ cup cooked oatmeal
- 3 cups air-popped popcorn
- ½ cup cooked quinoa
- 2 tablespoons raisins
- ½ medium sweet potato
- 1 slice 100% whole-wheat bread
- ⅓ cup cooked whole-wheat pasta
- ½ whole-wheat pita bread
- ½ whole-wheat English muffin
- ¼ cup dried, unsweetened fruit

Please note that since the above quantities are estimates, if you have type 1 diabetes or are taking insulin, you may need to be more precise in your carbohydrate counting by weighing and/or measuring your food.

None of these will raise your blood sugar, but they will all greatly enhance the taste of your food.

Enjoy your food. It may seem overly simple, but sitting down at a distraction-free table will also help you eat more balanced meals, because you will learn to enjoy your food more. This simple habit will encourage you to eat more slowly, notice when you are satisfied, and promote a positive relationship with food.

Get in the Kitchen

If you know how to cook, then you are already at an advantage! I always tell my clients that one of the best things my mom ever taught me was how to cook. On the other hand, if you aren't used to cooking yet, it's never too late! You will be glad to know that cooking for diabetes-friendly meals doesn't have to be

Type 1 and Type 2 Diabetes

Since type 1 diabetes is an autoimmune disease requiring insulin management, it is important to realize that individuals with this condition may need to pay extra attention to the quantity of total carbohydrates their meals contain, since this dictates how much insulin they give themselves. For this reason, you will see that each recipe provides the exact number of carbohydrates in the dish in an effort to arm you with all the information you need to best manage your diabetes. While eating balanced meals is just as significant with type 1 diabetes, we know that unexpected fluctuations in blood sugar are often reported due to the nature of the disease. For this reason, it is recommended that you seek out the expertise of a certified personal diabetes educator and registered dietitian to help customize your plan for your individual needs.

With type 2 diabetes, your body is having difficulty with the insulin that is created. There may not be enough insulin, or for some reason your body may have a problem utilizing the insulin produced. It is more common for individuals with type 2 diabetes to be overweight at the time of diagnosis, so it is encouraging to know that simply losing 5 to 10 percent of your body weight will usually result in an improvement in blood sugar due to an increase in insulin sensitivity. This is another reason the balanced-plate method will work, since a secondary benefit is that it will keep calories controlled as well.

complicated. You will notice that these recipes are simple and do not require too many ingredients. They do, however, require you to get in the kitchen, and I think you'll learn to love it! When you prepare your meals at home, you benefit in multiple ways: You know exactly what goes into your food, you have the ability to tweak recipes to your preferences, and you can serve yourself the correct portion sizes.

STOCKING YOUR PANTRY

I like to encourage individuals to look at their pantries as part of their success plan to managing their diabetes. You will feel better prepared when you strategically stock your pantry with food for your weekly meals as well as "backup" meals—meals you can swap in at any time if for any reason your originally planned meals are not possible. I have found this to be especially helpful if I come home and want to make something other than what I had planned for that day. Here is a list of the foods I always have on hand that can be thrown together at the last minute to prepare a quick and easy meal:

- Canned beans
- Canned tuna or salmon
- Dried fruit
- Lentils
- Nuts
- Oats
- Quinoa
- Whole-wheat crackers

While stocking your pantry for success, you will also want to make sure that it isn't filled with temptations. I have found that removing packaged snack foods further helps support healthy eating by inspiring us to get more creative in the kitchen and learn to whip up simple snacks and meals when we get hungry.

EQUIPMENT

The recipes in this book don't require a lot of fancy equipment. Most items you'll already have in your kitchen. But there are certain kitchen tools I wouldn't do without—they'll make your life a lot easier, while increasing your enjoyment of the whole cooking experience.

Slow cooker. This is a must for anyone with a busy schedule. There is no better feeling than coming home to a warm, nutritious meal that you didn't have to spend lots of time preparing. My basic formula for weeknight meals in a slow cooker is a protein + vegetables + seasoning. When I'm in the mood for a stew or soup, I simply add more liquid.

Food processor. I use my food processor every day. If you aren't a vegetable lover (yet!), this is a great way to start including more vegetables in whatever you are eating. Blend veggies in your food processor, then throw them into your scrambled eggs, smoothies, soups, casseroles . . . whatever you are eating. Doing this helps boost the fiber and nutrient content of anything!

Mason jars. While not exactly a piece of equipment, these multifunctional containers will help make your food prep easier and kitchen organization more streamlined. You can use them to store salads, homemade sauces, leftovers, overnight oats . . . you name it! I love that they are made of glass, so you can see exactly what they contain. You can also reheat leftovers in them, which is always a helpful time-saver.

About the Recipes

The recipes in this book were developed with the comfort-food lover in mind—after all, shouldn't we all be able to enjoy our food *while* improving our health? The recipes in this book will show you how to enjoy seemingly guilty pleasures like fried chicken, macaroni and cheese, and beef chili. When it comes to allowing yourself the foods you want, learning alternative ways to prepare them can often make all the difference. My hope is that you will take what you have learned in this chapter and see how I have applied these principles in the following recipes. With this knowledge you should feel confident experimenting in your own kitchen as you learn to create your own balanced plates.

The variety of recipes will show you how to make nourishing main dishes, as well as comforting side dishes and everything in between. I will show you how to put them together to create the balance your body needs and your taste buds crave.

You will find detailed nutritional information for each recipe that not only indicates the amount of carbohydrates in each serving but also highlights the overall nutritional benefits of each dish. You can use this information to ensure the recipes are meeting your personal needs based on the current management of your diabetes.

Popular Low-Carb Substitutions

You might be surprised that many delicious food swaps can help cut carbs in your favorite recipes. Using low-carb veggies as substitutes for traditional ingredients like pasta, rice, or potatoes allows you to continue enjoying the comfort foods you crave. And the best part? These substitutions don't require any sacrifice of flavor or satisfaction! Here are some of my favorites:

"Zoodles." Pick up some zucchini next time you're at the market and slice it thinly to substitute for lasagna noodles, or use a spiralizer to get even thinner "noodles" and mix them with your favorite marinara or pesto sauce. You can expect to save 45 to 60 grams of carbohydrates per cup.

Spaghetti squash. I love to use spaghetti squash instead of pasta. Try it in your favorite warm casserole or in a simple Italian dish. It will save you 20 to 25 grams of carbs per cup.

Cauliflower. There are so many possibilities for this versatile vegetable, because cauliflower can take on the flavors of whatever seasonings you choose to add. If you are making mashed potatoes, try substituting steamed cauliflower for half of the potatoes. You will save 15 grams of carbohydrates per cup. Or try cauliflower rice, a great side dish to top with your favorite lean protein. Simply pulse raw cauliflower in a food processor, and steam or sauté it in olive oil. This simple swap will save 45 grams of carbohydrates per cup.

Nonstarchy vegetables. If you usually pair your favorite dips with saltine crackers or white bread, simply swapping those refined carbs with vegetables can help make a huge improvement in your diabetes management. Try dipping cut-up carrots, cucumbers, or celery to save an easy 15 to 30 grams of carbohydrates per slice of bread or serving of crackers. Bonus: The vegetables contain extra fiber that will help keep you full longer and prevent spikes in your blood sugar.

Almond flour. Experiment with replacing the all-purpose flour called for in your favorite baking recipes with almond flour—or just start out by replacing half of it. This can save you 25 to 50 grams of carbohydrates per half serving.

FULL PLATE

**¼ PLATE
(PROTEIN)**

**¼ PLATE
(STARCH)**

**½ PLATE
(PROTEIN +
STARCH)**

**¾ PLATE
(VEG + STARCH)**

**¾ PLATE
(VEG + PROTEIN)**

**½ PLATE
(VEG)**

SIMPLE ICONS

The icons that you will notice next to each recipe indicate which element each recipe fulfills in the balanced-plate strategy. This visual will help guide you to the best options for creating your ideal complete meal. Some main dishes will be complete meals in themselves, while others will just fulfill the protein component of a balanced meal and would benefit from the addition of vegetable and starch side dishes.

COMPLETE THE PLATE

If a single recipe does not contain all the elements of a balanced plate, you will find additional suggestions for how best to complete it. Each meal you consume throughout the day should include the same breakdown: ½ nonstarchy vegetables, ¼ healthy protein, and ¼ carbohydrates. Even though it can be challenging to eat the recommended ½ plate of non-starchy vegetables at breakfast, I have still included the plate icons in the breakfast chapter to help ensure that you consume the appropriate amount of carbohydrates, protein, and healthy fat. Use this as a simple guide to help you assess how well this meets the plate method recommendations, but also realize you can adjust according to your personal needs. If a recipe contains only one or two of the three elements needed, be sure to add the additional element so that you complete your plate.

MIX AND MATCH MENUS

This book is laid out to inspire creativity in the kitchen, so feel free to mix and match the recipes to meet your preferences. The potential for trying different recipes together is what makes this book unique. I hope you will love the endless variety of possibilities this provides so you can truly eat what you love while improving your blood sugar levels and successfully managing your diabetes.

Chickpea Waffles with
Chia Seed Yogurt

Balanced Breakfasts

We all know that breakfast is an essential component of a healthy day, and this is especially true for those with diabetes. However, breakfast preparation often seems to take more time than we'd like. Thankfully, this doesn't have to be the case. The recipes here range from quick dishes you can make the night before and grab on your way out the door to those that take a little longer to prepare and are meant to be enjoyed on a leisurely weekend. Regardless of your time restraints, you will find a recipe that meets your needs.

Research has proven that eating a protein-rich breakfast can increase metabolism and help manage cravings all day long. In short, balanced breakfasts are an important element when it comes to controlling blood sugar. I hope you will try these recipes and find your personal favorites to provide the energy boost you need in the morning, while managing your diabetes throughout the day.

Pumpkin-Spice Muffins

SERVES 12 (1 MUFFIN EACH) Pumpkin shouldn't be reserved for only the Thanksgiving meal. With so many powerful nutrients, it's a terrific ingredient year-round. Pumpkin contains vitamin A, which helps promote healthy vision and immune systems, and is a great source of iron and magnesium. It's also low in calories and fat, so enjoy!

Nonstick cooking spray (optional)

2 cups oat flour (make your own by pulsing rolled oats in a food processor)

1 teaspoon baking soda

1 teaspoon baking powder

½ teaspoon ground cinnamon

¼ teaspoon ground nutmeg

¼ teaspoon salt

1 (15-ounce) can 100% pumpkin purée

2 large eggs, beaten

2 tablespoons honey

½ cup raisins

¼ PLATE

PREP TIME:
15 minutes

COOK TIME:
15 minutes

PER SERVING:
Calories: 124
Total fat: 2g
Saturated fat: <1g
Cholesterol: 27mg
Sodium: 283mg
Carbs: 23g
Fiber: 3g
Sugars: 8g
Protein: 4g

1. Preheat the oven to 350°F. Line the cups of a muffin tin with paper liners or lightly coat with nonstick cooking spray.

2. In a mixing bowl, combine the oat flour, baking soda, baking powder, cinnamon, nutmeg, and salt and mix well. Create a well in the middle of the mixture and add the pumpkin, eggs, honey, and raisins. Mix until just blended, but do not overmix.

3. Fill each muffin cup halfway full.

4. Bake until a toothpick inserted in the middle of a muffin comes out clean, about 15 minutes.

Tip: Be sure to buy pure pumpkin rather than pumpkin pie filling. This will ensure you get the vitamin A benefits without any added sugar. Each of these muffins will provide more than 65 percent of your daily vitamin A needs!

Complete the Plate: Add the Sunrise Frittata with Fresh Herbs (page 44) or Tomato, Onion, and Herb Omelet (page 48).

Yogurt, Berry, and Cinnamon-Pecan Parfait

FULL PLATE

PREP TIME:
10 minutes

PER SERVING:
Calories: 361
Total fat: 21g
Saturated fat: 2g
Cholesterol: 11mg
Sodium: 83mg
Carbs: 22g
Fiber: 6g
Sugars: 13g
Protein: 26g

SERVES 4 (1 PARFAIT EACH) Creamy Greek yogurt makes this easy breakfast feel decadent, which is the perfect way to start a day. Prep these parfaits the night before and have breakfast ready to go when you are. Nuts and yogurt combine for a filling, protein-packed punch, while the combination of antioxidant-rich berries delivers the sweetness you crave without piling on unnecessary fat and sugar.

1½ teaspoons ground cinnamon

2 tablespoons water

1 cup pecan pieces

4 cups plain nonfat Greek yogurt

1 cup fresh raspberries

1 cup fresh blueberries

1. In a small bowl, whisk the cinnamon into the water.

2. Heat a small skillet over medium heat. Add the pecans and pour the cinnamon mixture over them. Stir to coat. Cook, stirring frequently, until the water evaporates and the nuts are dry and toasted, about 7 minutes. Transfer to a plate and set aside.

3. Line up 4 parfait glasses, cups, or bowls on the counter. Portion out ½ cup of yogurt in each. Top with ¼ cup of raspberries. Add another ½ cup of yogurt. Top with ¼ cup of blueberries.

4. Top each parfait with ¼ cup of toasted pecan pieces. Serve.

Tip: If you prefer, you can make this recipe using frozen berries in place of fresh ones. When using frozen berries, make the parfait cups in advance, and refrigerate for at least 3 to 4 hours to allow the berries to thaw before serving.

Complete the Plate: While this makes a great meal on its own, you could still add a nonstarchy vegetable, Pumpkin-Spice Muffin (page 31), or Buckwheat-Apple Muffin (page 34).

eat what you love DIABETES COOKBOOK

Chocolate-Strawberry Breakfast Pudding

SERVES 2 (¾ CUP EACH) Dessert for breakfast? At first glance, this recipe might seem like an unlikely choice for the morning, but it's actually a great way to start your day. The combination of chia seeds and raspberries creates a high-fiber breakfast that will help stabilize your blood sugar while keeping you full throughout the morning. Since chia seeds are able to absorb 10 to 12 times their weight in water, they produce a pudding-like consistency that is both delicious and nutritious.

FULL PLATE

PREP TIME:
10 minutes +
30 minutes to chill

PER SERVING:
Calories: 219
Total fat: 13g
Saturated fat: 1g
Cholesterol: 0mg
Sodium: 97mg
Carbs: 23g
Fiber: 13g
Sugars: 6g
Protein: 6g

1 cup unsweetened almond milk

2 teaspoons pure maple syrup

½ teaspoon vanilla extract

¼ cup chia seeds

1½ teaspoon unsweetened cocoa powder

Dash ground cinnamon

½ cup fresh strawberries

1 tablespoon crushed almonds

1. Combine the almond milk, maple syrup, vanilla, chia seeds, cocoa, cinnamon, and strawberries in a blender. Pulse for 20 to 30 seconds.

2. Pour the mixture into a mason jar, cover, and refrigerate for at least 30 minutes, or longer if desired.

3. Divide the pudding between two bowls and top each with the almonds. Serve.

Tip: Strawberries are one of the highest-fiber fruits available, making them a great choice for individuals with diabetes. The high fiber content will prevent spikes in blood sugar, especially when paired with a protein source like the chia seeds and almonds featured here.

Complete the Plate: While this makes a great meal on its own, you could still add more to the meal if you desire or need. Other additions may include another serving of quality carbohydrates (15 grams), a non-starchy vegetable, or extra protein source, such as an omelet, frittata, chicken sausage, or simply a hardboiled egg.

Buckwheat-Apple Muffins

SERVES 12 (1 MUFFIN EACH) Buckwheat delivers a light nutty flavor, making it a great pairing in baked goods and a good stand-in for whole-wheat flour. Though its name would imply otherwise, buckwheat is not actually a wheat grain, and instead is gluten-free. Meanwhile, flaxseed meal and walnuts are superior sources of omega-3 fatty acids, and provide great crunchy texture in these simple muffins.

¼ PLATE

PREP TIME:
10 minutes

COOK TIME:
25 minutes

PER SERVING:
Calories: 137
Total fat: 10g
Saturated fat: 5g
Cholesterol: 14mg
Sodium: 93mg
Carbs: 13g
Fiber: 3g
Sugars: 5g
Protein: 3g

Nonstick cooking spray (optional)

¾ cup buckwheat flour

¼ cup flaxseed meal

1 teaspoon baking powder

¼ teaspoon salt

1 large egg

½ cup unsweetened almond milk

¼ cup coconut oil, melted

1 tablespoon honey

2 apples, cored, 1 diced and 1 sliced

½ cup walnut pieces

1. Preheat the oven to 350°F. Line the cups of a muffin tin with paper liners or lightly coat with nonstick cooking spray.

2. In a large mixing bowl, whisk together the buckwheat flour, flaxseed meal, baking powder, and salt.

3. In another bowl, whisk together the egg, almond milk, coconut oil, and honey. Fold the wet mixture into the dry mixture until just mixed. Stir in the diced apple and walnuts.

4. Spoon the batter into the muffin cups. Top each muffin with 1 or 2 apple slices.

5. Bake until browned and a toothpick inserted into the center of a muffin comes out clean, about 25 minutes. Cool for 10 minutes before serving.

Complete the Plate: Pair a muffin with a poached or hardboiled egg, Spinach and Swiss Crustless Quiche (page 51), or Tomato, Onion, and Herb Omelet (page 48).

Zucchini Nut Bread

SERVES 12 (1 SLICE EACH) Whether you are an experienced baker or a beginner, quick breads like this are very easy to master. Loaded with zucchini, walnuts, and chocolate chips, this dense bread is as filling as it is nutritious. Zucchini bread freezes wonderfully; simply wrap the cooled loaf in plastic wrap, place it in a zip-top plastic bag, and freeze for up to 3 months.

¼ PLATE

PREP TIME:
15 minutes

COOK TIME:
50 minutes

PER SERVING:
Calories: 159
Total fat: 10g
Saturated fat: 1g
Cholesterol: 14mg
Sodium: 113mg
Carbs: 17g
Fiber: 2g
Sugars: 5g
Protein: 4g

Nonstick cooking spray, for coating the loaf pan

1½ cups whole-wheat flour

½ teaspoon baking soda

⅛ teaspoon baking powder

¼ teaspoon salt

¼ teaspoon ground cinnamon

1 large egg

¼ cup unsweetened applesauce

¼ cup organic canola oil

2 tablespoons honey

2 tablespoons plain 2% Greek yogurt

1 cup shredded zucchini

½ cup chopped walnuts

2 tablespoons dark chocolate chips

1. Preheat the oven to 350ºF. Lightly coat an 8-by-4-inch loaf pan with nonstick cooking spray.

2. In a mixing bowl, combine the flour, baking soda, baking powder, salt, and cinnamon. Mix well.

3. In another bowl, whisk together the egg, applesauce, oil, honey, and yogurt. Fold the wet mixture into the dry mixture. Fold in the zucchini, walnuts, and chocolate chips.

4. Pour the batter into the prepared pan and bake until a toothpick inserted into the center comes out clean, about 50 minutes.

5. Let the loaf cool in the pan for 10 minutes. Then remove the loaf from the pan and cool completely on a wire rack.

Tip: Feel free to use other types of nuts if you prefer. Sliced almonds, pecans, and even macadamia nuts all work well for this dense, sweet loaf.

Complete the Plate: Serve with a hardboiled egg, Chocolate-Strawberry Breakfast Pudding (page 33), or Spinach and Swiss Crustless Quiche (page 51).

eat what you love DIABETES COOKBOOK

Blueberry-Mint Overnight Oats

SERVES 2 (½ CUP EACH) As I mentioned, eating breakfast is one of the best steps to take for managing both your blood sugar and overall health. If your mornings tend to be rushed, overnight oats are a great solution. Take a few minutes to prep the evening before, then grab your breakfast on the go. Oatmeal has always been one of the ultimate breakfast comfort foods, and this recipe can be served either warm or cold, whichever you prefer.

½ cup rolled oats

½ cup fresh blueberries

¼ cup plain nonfat Greek yogurt

½ cup unsweetened almond milk

1 teaspoon pure maple syrup

½ teaspoon vanilla extract

2 teaspoons chia seeds

2 fresh mint leaves, minced

½ teaspoon ground cinnamon

2 tablespoons crushed almonds

1. Combine the oats, blueberries, yogurt, almond milk, maple syrup, vanilla, chia seeds, mint, and cinnamon in a mason jar. Stir to combine, cover, and refrigerate overnight.

2. Divide the mixture between two bowls. If desired, heat for 30 to 60 seconds in the microwave. Top each serving with 1 tablespoon of crushed almonds. Enjoy!

Complete the Plate: This meal includes the proper amount of both carbohydrates and protein. It can be challenging to eat vegetables at breakfast, so any vegetables you're able to add would be a bonus!

½ PLATE

PREP TIME:
10 minutes +
overnight to chill

PER SERVING:
Calories: 193
Total fat: 7g
Saturated fat: 1g
Cholesterol: 1mg
Sodium: 57mg
Carbs: 27g
Fiber: 6g
Sugars: 7g
Protein: 8g

Whole-Grain Pancakes with Triple-Berry Chia Jam

FULL PLATE

PREP TIME:
10 minutes

COOK TIME:
10 minutes

PER SERVING:
Calories: 386
Total fat: 17g
Saturated fat: 4g
Cholesterol: 59mg
Sodium: 324mg
Carbs: 49g
Fiber: 11g
Sugars: 9g
Protein: 15g

SERVES 4 (2 PANCAKES EACH + 1 TABLESPOON JAM) Pancakes are a quint-essential breakfast food, and this multigrain version delivers comforting flavor without overstepping your eating plan. Buckwheat flour gives the pancakes a light nutty taste, which pairs wonderfully with this simple triple-berry chia jam that easily takes the place of syrup. This jam is so quick to whip up, I also like to use it on whole-wheat toast, or to create a more delicious version of the classic peanut butter and jelly sandwich. Feel free to change the berry combinations if you prefer. As long as you have 2 cups of berries total, it will come out perfect every time!

FOR THE JAM

1 cup fresh blackberries

½ cup fresh strawberries

½ cup fresh blueberries

1 tablespoon chia seeds

FOR THE PANCAKES

1 cup whole-wheat flour

¼ cup buckwheat flour

2 tablespoons flaxseed meal

1 teaspoon baking powder

¼ teaspoon salt

1 large egg

2 tablespoons unsweetened almond milk

1 tablespoon organic canola oil

1 tablespoon honey

1 cup plus 2 tablespoons plain 2% yogurt

Nonstick cooking spray

TO MAKE THE JAM

1. Heat a medium saucepan over medium-low heat. Add all the berries and cook, stirring and gently smashing the berries until they have broken down, 5 to 7 minutes.

2. Turn off the heat and stir in the chia seeds. Let the jam rest for 10 minutes before serving.

TO MAKE THE PANCAKES

1. In a mixing bowl, whisk together the whole-wheat flour, buckwheat flour, flaxseed, baking powder, and salt.

2. In another bowl, whisk together the egg, almond milk, canola oil, and honey. Add the yogurt and mix well. Fold the wet mixture into the dry mixture, stirring to combine.

3. Lightly coat a large skillet or griddle with nonstick cooking spray and heat over medium-high heat. Drop scant ¼-cup portions of the batter into the skillet (you will need to work in batches). Use the back of a spoon to spread the batter into circles 4 inches in diameter.

4. When small bubbles begin to form on the top, use a spatula to flip the pancakes. Continue to cook until set, 1 to 2 more minutes. Transfer the pancakes to a plate and cover with a clean kitchen towel to keep warm until the remaining pancakes are cooked. Serve with the chia jam.

Tip: Chia seeds are a member of the mint family and used as a thickener in many products because of their naturally gelatinous properties when mixed with a liquid. High in omega-3 fatty acids, they are a great substitute for poppy or sesame seeds, and can be found in most grocery stores or ordered online.

Millet Muesli with Citrus Fruits and Banana

SERVES 6 (⅓ CUP MUESLI + 6 SLICES FRUIT EACH) This simple muesli combines the filling grains millet and oats with naturally sweet coconut for an easy and appealing breakfast. Slightly sweet, the muesli pairs well with plain yogurt, kefir, or almond milk. Consider doubling the batch so you'll have plenty on hand for breakfasts all week, or enjoy a handful as a quick snack on the go.

¼ cup millet

½ cup boiling water

1 cup rolled oats

½ cup walnut pieces

¼ cup unsweetened coconut flakes

2 teaspoons honey

1½ teaspoons coconut oil, melted

1 teaspoon vanilla extract

¼ teaspoon salt

1 orange, divided into sections

1 grapefruit, divided into sections

½ banana, sliced

1. In a small bowl, combine the millet and boiling water. Cover and set aside for 30 minutes, then drain any excess water.

2. Preheat the oven to 325ºF.

3. In a large bowl, mix the cooked millet, oats, walnuts, and coconut flakes.

4. In a small bowl, mix the honey, oil, vanilla, and salt. Stir this mixture into the dry mixture. Spread out the muesli in a thin layer on a baking sheet.

5. Bake for 10 minutes, stir the muesli well, and continue to bake for an additional 10 minutes. Cool for 10 minutes before serving.

6. Serve in bowls, topped with the orange, grapefruit, and banana slices.

Complete the Plate: This meal needs protein and veggies, if possible. Serve with a hardboiled egg, a side of chicken sausage, or Spinach and Swiss Crustless Quiche (page 51).

¼ PLATE

PREP TIME:
10 minutes +
30 minutes to rest

COOK TIME:
20 minutes

PER SERVING:
Calories: 229
Total fat: 12g
Saturated fat: 5g
Cholesterol: 0mg
Sodium: 99mg
Carbs: 28g
Fiber: 5g
Sugars: 9g
Protein: 5g

Chickpea Waffles with Chia Seed Yogurt

FULL PLATE

PREP TIME:
10 minutes

COOK TIME:
20 minutes

PER SERVING:
Calories: 366
Total fat: 22g
Saturated fat: 13g
Cholesterol: 3mg
Sodium: 439mg
Carbs: 28g
Fiber: 8g
Sugars: 6g
Protein: 16g

SERVES 4 (1 WAFFLE EACH) Homemade waffles can be light and fluffy with a crisp exterior, even when made with protein-packed chickpea flour. These waffles are eye-openingly good, and surprisingly easy to get right. Spotted with flaxseed meal, which adds fiber and omega-3 fatty acids, these waffles can easily replace your buttermilk version for the better. Skip the syrup, and instead top them with a tangy yogurt sauce that complements the vanilla flavor of the waffles.

2 tablespoons chia seeds

1 cup plain nonfat Greek yogurt

1½ cups chickpea flour

3 tablespoons flaxseed meal

2 teaspoons baking powder

¼ teaspoon salt

1 medium egg

1½ cups unsweetened almond milk

¼ cup coconut oil, melted

1 teaspoon vanilla extract

1. In a small bowl, stir the chia seeds into the yogurt. Set aside.

2. Preheat a waffle iron on high. Preheat the oven to its lowest setting (typically around 160°F).

3. In a mixing bowl, combine the chickpea flour, flaxseed meal, baking powder, and salt. Mix well.

4. In a small bowl, mix the egg, almond milk, coconut oil, and vanilla. Pour the wet mixture into the mixing bowl, and stir to combine.

5. Drop ¼-cup portions of the batter onto the hot waffle iron, close, and cook until the waffle easily pulls away from the iron when opened, 3 to 5 minutes.

6. Transfer each finished waffle to the rack in the oven to keep warm and crisp until serving time. Serve the waffles with the yogurt-chia mixture spooned over the top.

Tip: Chickpea flour is a great gluten-free flour substitute. You can find chickpea flour in most grocery stores or online.

eat what you love DIABETES COOKBOOK

Loaded Avocado Toast with Fresh Peaches

SERVES 2 (1 SLICE EACH + ½ PEACH) I first learned of the simple pleasure of avocado toast when visiting friends in South America, where it is a breakfast staple. Now a trendy meal here in the United States, it's a great option for a quick balanced breakfast before you head out the door. Ready in less than 5 minutes, it's perfect for hectic weekday mornings and will keep you focused and full for several hours.

2 teaspoons extra-virgin olive oil

2 large eggs

2 whole-wheat bread slices

½ medium avocado

Pinch garlic powder

Pinch red pepper flakes

Pinch freshly ground black pepper

1 peach, pitted and sliced

FULL PLATE

PREP TIME:
5 minutes

COOK TIME:
5 minutes

PER SERVING:
Calories: 302
Total fat: 19g
Saturated fat: 4g
Cholesterol: 208mg
Sodium: 216mg
Carbs: 24g
Fiber: 7g
Sugars: 8g
Protein: 12g

1. Heat the olive oil in a medium skillet over medium-high heat. Crack the eggs into the skillet and cook to the desired doneness, 3 to 5 minutes.

2. While the eggs are cooking, toast the bread.

3. Divide the avocado between the two slices of toast, and slightly mash the avocado into the toast. Top each with a fried egg. Season with garlic powder, red pepper flakes, and black pepper.

4. Serve with the peach slices.

Tip: Ready to eat your avocado, but it isn't quite ripe? You can speed up the ripening process! Simply place your unripe avocado in a brown paper bag along with an underripe banana. The banana gives off a natural plant-ripening agent called ethylene gas that will speed up the ripening process. Your avocado will be ready to eat in 24 to 48 hours!

Sunrise Frittata with Fresh Herbs

¾ PLATE

PREP TIME:
5 minutes

COOK TIME:
20 minutes

PER SERVING:
Calories: 207
Total fat: 15g
Saturated fat: 5g
Cholesterol:
325mg
Sodium: 184mg
Carbs: 4g
Fiber: 1g
Sugars: 2g
Protein: 15g

SERVES 4 (1 SLICE EACH) To me, this dish recalls lazy weekends spent sipping coffee and enjoying casual conversations with those I love. It is always a favorite at weekend brunch gatherings with friends and family. What could be better than a dish offering a perfect blend of flavor, comfort, and color?

1 tablespoon extra-virgin olive oil

5 asparagus spears, trimmed and cut into 1-inch pieces

1 scallion, chopped

6 large eggs

¼ cup water

1 tablespoon unsweetened almond milk

4 large fresh basil leaves, chopped

1 teaspoon chopped fresh thyme

1 teaspoon chopped fresh oregano

¼ teaspoon freshly ground black pepper

Pinch salt (optional)

½ cup cherry tomatoes, halved

2 ounces fresh mozzarella, cut into bite-size pieces, or 6 small mozzarella balls

1. Preheat the oven to 350°F.

2. Heat the olive oil over medium heat in a 10-inch oven-safe skillet (preferably cast iron).

3. Add the asparagus and scallion and cook for 1 to 2 minutes. Remove from the heat.

4. In a mixing bowl, beat the eggs with the water and almond milk. Stir in the basil, thyme, oregano, pepper, and salt (if using).

5. Add the cooked veggies to the egg mixture and mix well.

6. Pour the mixture into the skillet. Scatter the tomatoes and mozzarella evenly over the top. Bake until cooked through, 15 to 18 minutes. Cut into 4 slices and serve.

Tip: Egg yolks are an excellent source of vitamin D! Since many individuals with diabetes have low vitamin D stores, this recipe is a delicious way to increase your intake. Vitamin D plays a key role in cell growth, immunity, and especially bone health.

Complete the Plate: Add a Pumpkin-Spice Muffin (page 31), 1 cup fresh berries, 1 slice whole-wheat toast topped with Triple-Berry Chia Jam (page 38), a piece of whole fruit, 6 ounces plain Greek yogurt, or ½ cup oatmeal.

Egg and Spinach Breakfast Burrito with Fresh Tomato Salsa

FULL PLATE

PREP TIME:
20 minutes

COOK TIME:
5 minutes

PER SERVING:
Calories: 287
Total fat: 11g
Saturated fat: 3g
Cholesterol:
216mg
Sodium: 637mg
Carbs: 35g
Fiber: 6g
Sugars: 6g
Protein: 15g

SERVES 4 (1 BURRITO EACH) Breakfast burritos are a great way to pack some extra leafy green vegetables into your diet first thing in the morning. Spinach is high in lutein, a phytonutrient that helps reduce inflammation and protect the eyes. It is quick cooking and blends wonderfully with savory Cheddar cheese, creating a simple and flavorful meal the whole family will enjoy. Prepare the salsa up to one day in advance for easy morning prep.

FOR THE SALSA

1 pound cherry or grape tomatoes

½ cup chopped scallions (green and white parts)

2 small jalapeños, seeded and minced

1 garlic clove, minced

⅛ teaspoon salt

Juice of 2 small limes

FOR THE BURRITOS

4 large eggs

⅛ teaspoon salt

¼ teaspoon freshly ground black pepper

1 teaspoon extra-virgin olive oil

5 ounces baby spinach

4 whole-wheat tortillas

¼ cup shredded sharp Cheddar cheese

1 avocado, pitted, peeled, and sliced (optional)

TO MAKE THE SALSA

In a small bowl, toss together all the ingredients. Cover and refrigerate until ready to serve.

TO MAKE THE BURRITOS

1. In a small bowl, beat the eggs with the salt and pepper.

2. In a small nonstick skillet, heat the olive oil over medium heat. Add the spinach and sauté briefly, until just wilted.

3. Pour the eggs into the pan and scramble, stirring regularly, until cooked through, 3 to 4 minutes.

4. Add one-quarter of the egg mixture to each tortilla and sprinkle with 1 table-spoon of cheese. If using, add a few avocado slices on top of the egg mixture. Fold the two sides in, then roll up the burrito. Serve with the salsa.

Tip: In the spring, when fresh greens are abundant, consider swapping out the spinach for a spicier green, such as arugula or watercress, for a bolder flavor.

Tomato, Onion, and Herb Omelet

¾ PLATE

PREP TIME:
10 minutes

COOK TIME:
5 minutes

PER SERVING:
Calories: 232
Total fat: 16g
Saturated fat: 4g
Cholesterol:
319mg
Sodium: 319mg
Carbs: 8g
Fiber: 2g
Sugars: 4g
Protein: 15g

SERVES 1 In this Mediterranean-inspired omelet, eggs are topped with a simple combination of tomatoes and red onion and seasoned with fresh basil leaves. Omelets require a slow, low heat to set while still maintaining a soft, fluffy texture, so keep an eye on this one throughout the cooking process to be sure to get the eggs just right.

2 large eggs

Dash salt

Dash freshly ground black pepper

1 teaspoon extra-virgin olive oil

½ cup chopped grape tomatoes

¼ cup thinly sliced red onion

2 or 3 fresh basil leaves, minced

1. In a small bowl, beat the eggs and season with salt and pepper.

2. In a small skillet, heat the olive oil over medium heat. Pour the eggs into the skillet and cook undisturbed until just set, 1 to 2 minutes. Use a spatula to loosen the edges of the omelet, and tilt the pan slightly to move any unset egg to the surface.

3. When the surface of the omelet is barely moist, scatter the tomatoes and onion over the top. Cover the pan, reduce the heat to low, and continue to cook for 1 minute. Remove the pan from the heat and let the omelet rest for about 1 minute, covered. Sprinkle with the basil and serve.

Complete the Plate: While this makes a filling meal on its own, you could also add a nonstarchy vegetable or starch/carbohydrate source such as a Pumpkin-Spice Muffin (page 31), Zucchini Nut Bread (page 36), or a Buckwheat-Apple Muffin (page 34).

Open-Faced Breakfast Tacos

FULL PLATE

PREP TIME:
5 minutes

COOK TIME:
15 minutes

PER SERVING:
Calories: 423
Total fat: 15g
Saturated Fat: 4g
Cholesterol:
416mg
Sodium: 186mg
Carbs: 48g
Fiber: 14g
Sugars: 4g
Protein: 25g

SERVES 2 (2 TACOS EACH) This complete meal is quick, easy, flavorful, and filling! Since I usually have all the ingredients on hand, and it's a simple recipe to adapt to the preferences of others, it has become one of my favorite breakfasts. Feel free to add chicken, substitute egg whites, make it extra spicy . . . whatever meets your needs!

Nonstick cooking spray, for coating the baking sheet

1 cup cooked or canned black beans, rinsed and drained

½ cup chopped tomato

½ cup chopped green bell pepper

4 tablespoons chopped red onion, divided

1 teaspoon minced jalapeño

Juice of 1 lime

1 teaspoon extra-virgin olive oil

4 organic corn tortillas

4 large eggs

Freshly ground black pepper

2 tablespoons chopped fresh cilantro

Dash hot sauce (optional)

Avocado slices (optional)

1. Preheat the oven to 350°F. Lightly coat a baking sheet with nonstick cooking spray.

2. In a small bowl, toss together the beans, tomato, bell pepper, 2 tablespoons of red onion, the jalapeño, lime juice, and oil.

3. Lay out the tortillas on the prepared baking sheet. Spoon an equal portion of the bean mixture on each tortilla. Create a shallow "nest" in the mixture on each tortilla and crack an egg into it. Sprinkle each egg with pepper.

4. Bake for 15 to 17 minutes, depending on how well you like the egg yolk to be cooked.

5. Top with the remaining 2 tablespoons of chopped onions and the cilantro. Add hot sauce and/or avocado (if using).

eat what you love DIABETES COOKBOOK

Spinach and Swiss Crustless Quiche

SERVES 5 (2 SLICES EACH) Quiche is traditionally prepared with a butter crust, which packs on carbohydrates and fat. This simple crustless quiche, on the other hand, demands less prep work and boasts the same comforting results. Spinach and bell peppers add fiber to the dish, and Swiss cheese contributes a deep, savory flavor to make this a breakfast favorite that is both filling and easy to prepare in advance for those busy mornings.

¾ PLATE

PREP TIME:
10 minutes
COOK TIME:
45 minutes

PER SERVING:
Calories: 251
Total fat: 17g
Saturated fat: 7g
Cholesterol:
435mg
Sodium: 458mg
Carbs: 4g
Fiber: 1g
Sugars: 2g
Protein: 20g

Nonstick cooking spray, for coating the pie dish

10 large eggs

½ cup unsweetened almond milk

¾ cup finely diced Swiss cheese

2 cups chopped spinach

1 red bell pepper, seeded and diced

1 teaspoon dried thyme

½ teaspoon salt

¼ teaspoon freshly ground black pepper

1. Preheat the oven to 350ºF. Lightly coat a 9-inch pie dish with nonstick cooking spray.

2. In a large bowl, beat the eggs. Stir in the almond milk, cheese, spinach, bell pepper, thyme, salt, and black pepper. Pour the mixture into the prepared pie dish.

3. Bake until a knife inserted in the center comes out clean, about 45 minutes. Cool for 20 minutes before slicing and serving.

Tip: This quiche can be prepared up to one day in advance. Cook and cool the quiche, then cover it with aluminum foil and refrigerate. When you're ready to eat, reheat it for 15 minutes at 350ºF.

Complete the Plate: Add a starchy vegetable like a small baked sweet potato, a Pumpkin-Spice Muffin (page 31), Zucchini Nut Bread (page 36), or a Buckwheat-Apple Muffin (page 34).

Crispy Classic Chilaquiles

SERVES 2 (1 CUP EACH) Looking to spice up your breakfast? If so, look no further! Incorporating vegetables into the first meal of the day isn't always easy, but chilaquiles can do the trick. Meanwhile, the flavors in this recipe combine well to create a traditional, comforting Mexican meal. For extra protein, I also like topping this dish with a fried egg. The egg will not only complete your plate but also keep you satisfied for hours to come.

FULL PLATE

PREP TIME:
10 minutes

COOK TIME:
20 minutes

PER SERVING:
Calories: 291
Total fat: 11g
Saturated fat: 2g
Cholesterol: 41mg
Sodium: 403mg
Carbs: 32g
Fiber: 5g
Sugars: 6g
Protein: 19g

4 organic corn tortillas

3 teaspoons extra-virgin olive oil, divided

Freshly ground black pepper

2 medium tomatoes, sliced

2 tablespoons diced green chiles

2 garlic cloves, peeled

½ cup diced onion

½ cup shredded cooked chicken

¼ cup chopped fresh cilantro

Avocado slices (optional)

1 teaspoon grated Parmesan cheese (optional)

2 tablespoons minced jalapeños (optional)

1. Preheat the oven to 350ºF. Line a baking sheet with aluminum foil.

2. Slice the tortillas into 1-inch strips, then slice in the opposite direction to make bite-size pieces.

3. Put the tortilla pieces on the lined baking sheet. Drizzle with 2 teaspoons of olive oil and toss to blend evenly. Arrange in a single layer and lightly sprinkle with pepper. Bake until the tortillas are crisp, 12 to 13 minutes.

4. While the tortillas are baking, add the tomatoes, chiles, and garlic cloves to a food processor and blend until smooth, 20 to 30 seconds.

5. Heat the remaining 1 teaspoon of olive oil over medium heat in a medium skillet. Add the onion and sauté until slightly browned, 2 to 3 minutes.

6. Add the tomato mixture to the skillet, reduce the heat to medium-low, and simmer until the mixture thickens slightly, 2 to 3 minutes.

7. Add the tortilla strips and shredded chicken and stir to mix well. Cook until all the ingredients are warmed through, 2 minutes or so. Remove from the heat.

8. Divide the chilaquiles between two bowls. Top each portion with cilantro and avocado, Parmesan cheese, and jalapeños (if using).

Classic Cobb Salad

Poultry Mains

My favorite part about working with individuals with diabetes is showing them how they can enjoy the foods they love without ever having to sacrifice flavor. When I help people realize that not only can they still look forward to every meal but also that what they eat can actually help improve their blood sugar . . . that's usually when the real progress begins! Food can be a tool to help you manage your diabetes for the rest of your life. If this is the case, shouldn't it taste amazing? I believe so!

In this chapter, I've included all the classic, comforting poultry dishes you crave—chicken pot pie, creamy casseroles, and even chicken noodle soup. These wholesome meals will provide all you could ask for to treat your taste buds every day of the week!

Skillet Chicken with Asparagus and Quinoa

SERVES 4 (1 CUP EACH) This was one of the first recipes I created when I began developing healthier methods of preparing traditional comfort foods. Since turmeric boasts such major health benefits (see the Tip), it seemed like a great place to start. What I love most about turmeric is that it doesn't have an overpowering taste and blends nicely with other flavors.

FULL PLATE

PREP TIME:
10 minutes

COOK TIME:
25 minutes

PER SERVING:
Calories: 257
Total fat: 8g
Saturated fat: <1g
Cholesterol: 61mg
Sodium: 323mg
Carbs: 21g
Fiber: 4g
Sugars: 3g
Protein: 29g

1 pound asparagus, trimmed and cut into 1-inch pieces

1 tablespoon plus 1 teaspoon extra-virgin olive oil, divided

⅛ teaspoon salt

¼ teaspoon freshly ground black pepper

1 cup water

½ cup quinoa, rinsed and drained

1 pound boneless, skinless chicken breasts, cut into 2-inch pieces

1 tablespoon ground turmeric

2 cups chopped spinach

2 tablespoons balsamic vinegar

½ teaspoon garlic powder

¼ cup feta cheese (optional)

1. Preheat the oven to 400°F. Line a baking sheet with parchment paper.

2. Spread out the asparagus on the baking sheet and toss with 1 teaspoon of olive oil. Season with the salt and pepper. Bake for 10 minutes, stirring once.

3. Meanwhile, in a small saucepan, bring the water to a boil over medium-high heat. Add the quinoa, reduce the heat to low, cover, and cook for 15 minutes. When the quinoa is done, all the water should be evaporated.

4. While the quinoa is cooking, heat the remaining 1 tablespoon of olive oil in a large skillet over medium-high heat. Add the chicken and turmeric. Sauté until cooked through, 4 to 5 minutes per side. ▶

5. Add the cooked asparagus to the quinoa, along with the chopped spinach, chicken, balsamic vinegar, and garlic powder and stir to combine.

6. Sprinkle the feta cheese on top (if using). Serve warm.

Tip: Studies have shown that the curcumin found in turmeric has anti-inflammatory properties and may even be helpful in preventing cancer. Piperine, a compound found in black pepper, is able to help increase the absorption of turmeric to create this tasty, disease-fighting comfort food!

Complete the Plate: While this dish has all of the important elements of a balanced plate, it would be helpful to add another vegetable side to increase your fiber intake. Try adding the Sautéed Garlic, Ginger, and Shallot Green Beans (page 156) or Five-Minute Brussels Sprouts and Almonds (page 154).

Southern Chicken Salad

SERVES 4 (1 CUP EACH) When I was growing up in the South, my mom made the best chicken salad! Considering she served it to celebrate so many different occasions—baby showers, summer barbecues, church potlucks, family dinners—it's hardly a surprise that chicken salad is the definition of comfort food to me. However, all that mayo is not good for anyone, so I've made a simple swap for Greek yogurt. It still has all the creaminess you want, without sacrificing flavor. This is indeed a dish worth bringing out on celebratory occasions, so I hope you will use it this way as well.

¾ PLATE

PREP TIME:
10 minutes

COOK TIME:
25 minutes

PER SERVING:
Calories: 224
Total fat: 10g
Saturated fat: 2g
Cholesterol: 64mg
Sodium: 347mg
Carbs: 10g
Fiber: 2g
Sugars: 7g
Protein: 27g

1 pound boneless, skinless chicken breasts

¾ cup chopped spinach

½ cup diced celery

½ cup red grapes, quartered

¼ cup chopped pecans

2 tablespoons dried cherries or raisins

½ cup plain 2% Greek yogurt

½ teaspoon poultry seasoning

¼ teaspoon onion powder

¼ teaspoon freshly ground black pepper

⅛ teaspoon salt

1. Bring a large pot of water to a boil over medium-high heat. Add the chicken and cook for 25 minutes.

2. With a slotted spoon, transfer the chicken to a large mixing bowl; reserve ¼ cup of the cooking liquid. Once the chicken is cool enough to handle, shred it into small pieces with your fingers. Add the reserved cooking liquid.

3. Add the remaining ingredients and mix to combine. Enjoy!

Tip: Magnesium is a very important mineral for individuals with diabetes because it helps regulate blood sugar. This recipe is rich in magnesium, thanks to the spinach and pecans.

Complete the Plate: Serve this chicken salad alongside a slice of whole-wheat bread or a few whole-wheat crackers, or with your favorite starch/grain side.

Perfect Mediterranean Chicken

¾ PLATE

PREP TIME:
10 minutes

COOK TIME:
40 minutes

PER SERVING:
Calories: 247
Total fat: 13g
Saturated Fat: 1g
Cholesterol: 61mg
Sodium: 377mg
Carbs: 12g
Fiber: 3g
Sugars: 3g
Protein: 26g

SERVES 4 (1 CHICKEN BREAST + 1½ CUPS VEGETABLES + 2½ TEASPOONS DRESSING EACH) Goodbye, bottled dressing . . . hello, healthy, homemade dressing! Many of the salad dressings you find in grocery stores contain added salt and other preservatives. Using a few simple ingredients, you can create your own healthy versions of dressing in a matter of seconds. The Mediterranean dressing is drizzled over tender chicken and vegetables here, but you can also enjoy it on your favorite protein, roasted vegetables, or green leafy salads.

FOR THE DRESSING

1 tablespoon extra-virgin olive oil

2 tablespoons balsamic vinegar

1 teaspoon honey

1 garlic clove, minced

FOR THE CHICKEN

2 teaspoons extra-virgin olive oil

4 boneless, skinless chicken breasts (about 1 pound)

Freshly ground black pepper

¼ cup black olives, drained, rinsed, and chopped

1 cup oil-packed sun-dried tomatoes, drained

1 cup asparagus pieces (2-inch pieces)

4 cups arugula

1 to 2 tablespoons grated Parmesan cheese (optional)

eat what you love DIABETES COOKBOOK

TO MAKE THE DRESSING

Whisk together the olive oil, vinegar, honey, and garlic. Set aside.

TO MAKE THE CHICKEN

1. Preheat the oven to 350ºF.

2. Heat the olive oil in a medium skillet over medium heat. Add the chicken and season with pepper. Cook until lightly browned on both sides, 4 to 5 minutes. Transfer the chicken to a glass baking dish and bake for 20 minutes.

3. Top the chicken with the olives, tomatoes, and asparagus. Continue to cook until an instant-read thermometer inserted into the thickest part of a breast reads 160ºF, 10 to 15 minutes.

4. Divide the arugula among four plates. Place a chicken breast and some vegetables over the arugula. Drizzle 2 to 3 teaspoons of the dressing over the chicken and vegetables. Sprinkle with Parmesan cheese (if using) and more black pepper, if desired.

Complete the Plate: Serve with ¾ cup of your favorite whole grain or a piece of whole fruit.

Classic Chicken Comfort Bowl

FULL PLATE

PREP TIME:
5 minutes

COOK TIME:
4 to 6 hours

PER SERVING:
Calories: 398
Total fat: 10g
Saturated fat: 1g
Cholesterol: 60mg
Sodium: 442mg
Carbs: 47g
Fiber: 15g
Sugars: 4g
Protein: 35g

SERVES 4 (3¼ CUPS EACH) Hardly a week goes by that you won't find this meal simmering in my slow cooker. Since it takes just a few minutes to prep and throw together in the morning, it's the perfect option for a busy lifestyle. The ingredients are kitchen staples I always have on hand, and the product is a satisfying family favorite! I often double the recipe so I can use the extra chicken throughout the week for breakfast tacos, salads, and even lettuce wraps.

1 pound boneless, skinless chicken breasts

½ cup salsa

1⅓ cups cooked brown rice

2 cups cooked or canned black beans, rinsed and drained

1 cup cherry tomatoes, quartered

¼ cup chopped red onion

4 cups romaine lettuce

1 avocado, pitted, peeled, and sliced

¼ cup chopped fresh cilantro

4 lime wedges

1. Put the chicken in the slow cooker and pour the salsa over it. Cover and cook on low for 4 to 6 hours.

2. Shred the chicken. Distribute the chicken, salsa, rice, beans, tomatoes, onion, lettuce, avocado, and cilantro evenly among four bowls. Squeeze the juice of one lime wedge over each bowl and serve.

Warm Honey-Balsamic Chicken Salad

SERVES 4 (1½ CUPS EACH) Simple, warm chicken recipes are my favorites. I find that quick marinades are the best way to lock in flavor while ensuring the chicken will be perfectly moist. The addition of a quality balsamic vinegar is key in this recipe, as it helps provide a sweet acidity alongside the honey, which enriches the entire dish. Feel free to grill your chicken if you prefer.

FULL PLATE

PREP TIME:
15 minutes +
30 minutes to
marinate

COOK TIME:
35 minutes

PER SERVING:
Calories: 372
Total fat: 12g
Saturated fat: 2g
Cholesterol: 61mg
Sodium: 299mg
Carbs: 36g
Fiber: 4g
Sugars: 6g
Protein: 33g

4 boneless, skinless chicken breasts (about 1 pound)

¼ cup aged balsamic vinegar

2 tablespoons extra-virgin olive oil

2 teaspoons honey

2 or 3 garlic cloves, minced

½ teaspoon freshly ground black pepper

1 cup uncooked quinoa

2 cups low-sodium chicken broth

4 cups spinach

Pinch salt, if desired

1. Put the chicken in a zip-top bag.

2. In a small bowl, whisk together the vinegar, oil, honey, garlic, and pepper. Pour half of the mixture into the bag with the chicken, seal it, and toss a few times to make sure the marinade is distributed over all the chicken. Refrigerate for at least 30 minutes. (Reserve the rest of the balsamic mixture for serving.)

3. Preheat the oven to 400°F.

4. Transfer the chicken to an 8-inch square baking dish. Bake until a thermometer inserted in a breast reads 165°F, 30 to 35 minutes.

5. While the chicken is in the oven, combine the quinoa and chicken broth in a small saucepan. Bring to a boil over medium-high heat, then reduce to a simmer, cover, and cook until the liquid is evaporated, about 15 minutes. Five minutes before the quinoa is done, add the spinach.

6. Serve the chicken on top of the quinoa and spinach mixture. Drizzle with the reserved balsamic mixture and a pinch of salt, if desired.

Complete the Plate: You can always add more vegetables, so if you are feeling hungry, consider adding another vegetable side dish.

Chipotle Chicken with Creamy Avocado-Lime Sauce

¼ PLATE

PREP TIME:
15 minutes +
30 minutes to
marinate

COOK TIME:
35 minutes

PER SERVING:
Calories: 242
Total fat: 15g
Saturated fat: 2g
Cholesterol: 61mg
Sodium: 309mg
Carbs: 5g
Fiber: 2g
Sugars: 2g
Protein: 24g

SERVES 4 (1 CHICKEN BREAST + 2 TABLESPOONS SAUCE EACH) Despite what you may think, Mexican food can be healthy, and this recipe will show you how! I like to double the recipe for the sauce and use it throughout the week as a veggie dip and salad dressing, and use it in other Mexican-inspired dishes. It is very versatile, so it makes a great addition to any lean protein.

FOR THE CHICKEN

4 boneless, skinless chicken breasts (about 1 pound)

2 tablespoons extra-virgin olive oil

1½ tablespoons freshly squeezed lime juice

1 teaspoon pure maple syrup

½ teaspoon chipotle chile powder

½ teaspoon garlic powder

Pinch salt

Pinch freshly ground black pepper

FOR THE CREAMY LIME SAUCE

½ ripe avocado, pitted and peeled

1 tablespoon chopped seeded jalapeño

1 garlic clove, peeled

1 tablespoon extra-virgin olive oil

¼ teaspoon grated lime zest

1½ tablespoons freshly squeezed lime juice

2 tablespoons chopped fresh cilantro

Pinch salt

Pinch freshly ground black pepper

1. Put the chicken in a zip-top bag.

2. In a small bowl, whisk together the olive oil, lime juice, maple syrup, chipotle chile powder, garlic powder, salt, and pepper. Add the marinade to the bag with the chicken, seal it, and toss a few times to make sure the marinade is distributed over all the chicken. Refrigerate for at least 30 minutes.

3. Preheat the oven to 400°F.

4. Remove the chicken from the marinade and transfer it to in an 8-inch square baking dish. Bake until a thermometer inserted in a breast reads 165°F, 30 to 35 minutes.

5. While the chicken is cooking, prepare the creamy lime sauce by combining all the ingredients in a food processor and processing until smooth. Top each serving of the chicken with 1 to 2 tablespoons of the creamy sauce.

Complete the Plate: Serve with your favorite vegetable side and starch/grain side. I love to add the Mexi-Cauli Rice (page 151) and 1 cup of black beans topped with fresh salsa.

Oven-Baked "Fried" Chicken

¼ PLATE

PREP TIME:
10 minutes

COOK TIME:
45 minutes

PER SERVING:
Calories: 190
Total fat: 5g
Saturated fat: 2g
Cholesterol: 86mg
Sodium: 445mg
Carbs: 5g
Fiber: 1g
Sugars: <1g
Protein: 13g

SERVES 4 (1 DRUMSTICK EACH) If you are a fan of fried chicken, it can be really hard to give up this classic comfort food when you embark on a plan of healthier eating. Don't worry, though, because you can replicate the flavor and crunch with this easy remake that will allow you to ditch the frying for an oven-baked alternative. Adding Parmesan cheese to the breading helps cut the carbs, while the combination brings added crunch to the drumsticks.

Nonstick cooking spray

4 chicken drumsticks, skin removed

½ teaspoon onion powder

½ teaspoon garlic powder

½ teaspoon salt

¼ teaspoon freshly ground black pepper

1 large egg

2 tablespoons unsweetened almond milk

¼ cup grated Parmesan cheese

4 tablespoons whole-wheat bread crumbs

1. Preheat the oven to 375°F. Coat a small baking pan with nonstick cooking spray.

2. Season the drumsticks with the onion powder, garlic powder, salt, and pepper.

3. In a shallow bowl, whisk together the egg and almond milk. In another shallow bowl, combine the Parmesan cheese and bread crumbs.

4. One by one, dip each drumstick into the egg mixture. Shake to let the excess drip off. Roll the drumsticks in the bread crumb mixture and place in the baking pan. ▶

5. Bake, turning the drumsticks over halfway through cooking, until the coating is browned and the juices run clear, about 45 minutes.

Tip: If you like your fried chicken spicy, add 2 tablespoons of your favorite hot sauce to the chicken in step 2 when you season the chicken, and let it rest for 20 minutes before proceeding. Shake off any excess hot sauce before dipping the chicken into the egg mixture, then proceed as directed.

Complete the Plate: Serve with a starchy side such as Mashed Cauliflower and Potatoes (page 170) or Macaroni and Cheese with Mixed Vegetables (page 178) and a Simple Green Salad with Garlic, Lemon, and Olive Oil Vinaigrette (page 145) or Sweet and Tender Kale Salad (page 143).

Ginger-Chicken Noodle Soup

SERVES 4 (1½ CUPS EACH) There are few soups that offer the comforting touch of a bowl of home-cooked chicken noodle soup. This simple version is loaded with ginger, a soothing spice that not only stimulates digestion and boosts circulation but also helps warm you up. Using chicken thighs gives you tender, flavorful meat, and because they are boneless, cooking time is minimal.

¾ PLATE

PREP TIME:
10 minutes

COOK TIME:
20 minutes

PER SERVING:
Calories: 329
Total fat: 21g
Saturated fat: 5g
Cholesterol: 95mg
Sodium: 343mg
Carbs: 11g
Fiber: 3g
Sugars: 3g
Protein: 26g

1 teaspoon organic canola oil

1 pound boneless, skinless chicken thighs, trimmed and cut into bite-size pieces

2 carrots, peeled and julienned

2 celery stalks, diced

4 scallions, thinly sliced (green and white parts)

2 garlic cloves, minced

4 cups low-sodium chicken broth

1 cup water

1 tablespoon low-sodium soy sauce

1-inch knob fresh ginger, peeled and grated

1½ cups shirataki noodles, drained (see Tip)

1. In a large Dutch oven, heat the oil over medium-high heat. Add the chicken pieces and cook, stirring frequently, until browned.

2. Add the carrots, celery, and scallions and continue to cook for 2 minutes, stirring regularly. Add the garlic and cook for 1 additional minute.

3. Add the chicken broth, water, soy sauce, and ginger. Cook for 10 minutes to let the flavors meld. Add the noodles and cook until heated through. Serve hot.

Tip: Shirataki noodles are made from the konjac yam and come in a variety of sizes. For this soup, a thick-cut, linguine-style noodle works best. These low-carbohydrate noodles are high in fiber and low in calories, making them a great option for soups and stews. Find shirataki noodles at well stocked grocery stores, health food stores, Asian markets, or online.

Complete the Plate: While this dish does contain some carbohydrates, it is still low in carbs. Feel free to add a serving of whole-grain crackers or a starch side along with another nonstarchy vegetable such as Vegetable Fried Cauliflower Rice (page 150) or Grilled Zucchini Salad (page 157).

Creamy Broccoli and Chicken Casserole

FULL PLATE

PREP TIME:
20 minutes

COOK TIME:
35 minutes

PER SERVING:
Calories: 396
Total fat: 17g
Saturated fat: 5g
Cholesterol:
106mg
Sodium: 448mg
Carbs: 24g
Fiber: 5g
Sugars: 2g
Protein: 39g

SERVES 4 (1½ CUPS EACH) There is nothing better than a creamy, warm casserole at the end of a long day. Admittedly, when I first learned how to cook, I only knew how to make sauces for my casseroles using canned soups. I'm so glad I eventually realized that creating my own sauce was not only easy but took no extra time in the kitchen! This casserole completes the entire plate, making it a one-pot dish to be enjoyed by the whole family.

Nonstick cooking spray

1 cup cooked quinoa (prepared with low-sodium chicken broth instead of water)

1 (16-ounce) bag frozen (thawed) broccoli or 2 cups fresh broccoli florets

2½ cups diced cooked chicken

2 cups unsweetened almond milk (I use Califia Farms brand)

¼ cup whole-wheat flour

¼ cup plain nonfat Greek yogurt

½ cup grated sharp Cheddar cheese

1 teaspoon garlic powder

¼ teaspoon salt

½ teaspoon freshly ground black pepper

Dash cayenne pepper

2 tablespoons walnuts

2 tablespoons grated Parmesan cheese

2 tablespoons whole-wheat bread crumbs

1 tablespoon extra-virgin olive oil

1. Preheat the oven to 375°F. Coat an 8-inch square baking dish with nonstick cooking spray.

2. Spread out the quinoa in the baking dish and cover with the broccoli and chicken.

eat what you love DIABETES COOKBOOK

3. In a medium saucepan set over medium-high heat, whisk together the almond milk and whole-wheat flour until slightly thickened, about 5 minutes. Add the Greek yogurt, Cheddar cheese, garlic powder, salt, black pepper, and cayenne pepper. Stir until everything is melted and combined, 1 to 2 minutes. Pour the mixture over the broccoli, chicken, and quinoa.

4. Combine the walnuts, Parmesan cheese, and bread crumbs in a food processor. Pulse 10 to 20 times, until a fine mixture is made. Add the olive oil and mix with your hands to create a crumble. Spread the crumble evenly over the broccoli mixture.

5. Bake for 30 minutes.

Tip: I prefer to use almond milk instead of cow's milk because it is much lower in carbohydrates. Whereas cow's milk contains 12 grams of carbohydrates per cup, almond milk only has 2 grams.

Chicken Pot Pie

FULL PLATE

PREP TIME:
25 minutes

COOK TIME:
35 minutes

PER SERVING:
Calories: 441
Total fat: 27g
Saturated fat: 13g
Cholesterol: 36mg
Sodium: 340mg
Carbs: 32g
Fiber: 4g
Sugars: 5g
Protein: 19g

SERVES 6 (1 SLICE EACH) Chicken pot pie is savory cool-weather fare that can't be beat. Combining vegetables and cooked chicken, this easy meal is filling and customizable to whatever vegetables you happen to have on hand. Using a single layer of crust instead of two allows you to significantly cut carbs while holding on to the most important layer—the flaky goodness of the top.

FOR THE FILLING

1 tablespoon extra-virgin olive oil

1 carrot, peeled and diced

1 celery stalk, diced

1 large onion, diced

2 cups shredded or diced cooked chicken

1 tablespoon whole-wheat flour

1¼ cups unsweetened almond milk

1 cup fresh or frozen green peas

½ teaspoon salt

½ teaspoon freshly ground pepper

FOR THE POT PIE

1⅓ cups whole-wheat flour

¼ teaspoon salt

⅓ cup extra-virgin olive oil

TO MAKE THE FILLING

1. In a large skillet, heat the oil over medium-high heat. Add the carrot, celery, and onion and cook, stirring frequently, until beginning to soften, 3 to 4 minutes.

2. Add the chicken and continue to stir. Sprinkle the flour over the chicken and vegetables and stir to mix evenly. Add the almond milk, green peas, salt, and pepper. Bring to a simmer and stir continuously until the liquid begins to thicken, about 2 minutes. Transfer the mixture to a 9-inch pie dish.

3. Preheat the oven to 350ºF.

TO MAKE THE POT PIE

1. In a mixing bowl, combine the flour and salt. Drizzle with the olive oil and stir to combine.

2. Fill a measuring cup with water and several ice cubes. Pour 2 tablespoons of the ice water into the flour mixture, stirring as you go. Continue stirring the flour and adding more ice water, 1 tablespoon at a time, until the dough comes together.

3. Shape the dough into a ball and press it flat into a disk. Place the disk between two sheets of lightly floured wax paper. Roll the dough into a 12-inch circle.

4. Transfer the dough to the pie dish containing the chicken, trim away any overhanging crust, and pinch the edges to seal. Cut a few vent slits in the dough to let steam escape.

5. Bake until the crust is lightly golden, about 30 minutes. Let sit for 15 minutes before serving.

Complete the Plate: Serve this with an additional vegetable dish such as Broccolini, Yellow Squash, and Radishes with a Mustard-Yogurt Dressing (page 153), Simple Green Salad with Garlic, Lemon, and Olive Oil Vinaigrette (page 145), or Grilled Zucchini Salad (page 157).

Barbecued Chicken Pizza with Red Peppers

SERVES 8 (1 SLICE EACH) Pizza is always a favorite comfort food, and can still be enjoyed even when watching your carb intake. Barbecued chicken is the star of the show in this simple variety, with an almond flour crust that keeps the carb count low. Be sure to use fresh mozzarella, which imparts a rustic look and loads of flavor. Look for a barbecue sauce that does not contain added sugar in the ingredients list—on the nutritional facts label, sugar should be less than 4 grams.

½ PLATE

PREP TIME:
10 minutes

COOK TIME:
30 minutes

PER SERVING:
Calories: 338
Total fat: 20g
Saturated fat: 4g
Cholesterol: 117mg
Sodium: 329mg
Carbs: 22g
Fiber: 5g
Sugars: 7g
Protein: 21g

FOR THE CRUST

1½ cups almond flour

¾ cup whole-wheat flour

2 tablespoons coconut flour

½ teaspoon baking powder

½ teaspoon salt

3 large eggs

2 tablespoons organic canola oil

FOR THE PIZZA

8 ounces boneless, skinless chicken breasts, cooked and shredded

½ cup barbecue sauce, divided

4 ounces fresh mozzarella cheese, thinly sliced

1 cup sliced red bell pepper

¼ cup chopped fresh cilantro

TO MAKE THE CRUST

1. Preheat the oven to 350°F.

2. In a mixing bowl, whisk together the almond flour, wheat flour, coconut flour, baking powder, and salt.

3. In a small bowl, whisk together the eggs and canola oil. Pour the wet mixture into the dry mixture and use your hands to mix the dough until it forms a ball. Press the ball into a disk.

4. Place the disk between two sheets of parchment paper. Roll out the dough into a large, flat circle. Remove the top sheet of parchment and transfer the dough and bottom sheet of parchment to a baking sheet. Bake until the edges are crisp, about 20 minutes. ▶

TO MAKE THE PIZZA

1. Toss the shredded chicken with ¼ cup of barbecue sauce.

2. Spread the remaining ¼ cup of barbecue sauce on the precooked pizza crust. Add the mozzarella slices to the pizza. Top with the shredded chicken and red bell pepper. Return the pizza to the oven and cook for 10 more minutes.

3. Let the pizza rest for 10 minutes. Top with the cilantro, slice, and serve.

Tip: Almond flour, also called almond meal, is made from ground almonds. It can be used for baking and is a great gluten-free and low-carb alternative. Find it at health food stores, well-stocked grocery stores, and online.

Complete the Plate: Pair with a Simple Green Salad with Garlic, Lemon, and Olive Oil Vinaigrette (page 145), Roasted Beets and Greens with Balsamic Dressing (page 161), or Broccolini, Yellow Squash, and Radishes with Mustard-Yogurt Dressing (page 153).

Classic Cobb Salad

SERVES 8 (1 CUP EACH) This hearty salad combines chicken and bacon, a super comfort-food duo. Topped off with healthy fats from avocado, it will have you abandoning any doubts about eating veggies for dinner.

FOR THE SALAD

6 turkey bacon slices

1 pound boneless, skinless chicken breasts

⅛ teaspoon salt

⅛ teaspoon freshly ground black pepper

2 cups baby spinach

6 cups romaine lettuce, cut into small chunks

1 avocado, pitted, peeled, and sliced

2 large eggs, hardboiled

1 cucumber, diced

½ cup cherry tomatoes

FOR THE DRESSING

⅔ cup extra-virgin olive oil

⅓ cup red wine vinegar

1 tablespoon Dijon mustard

1 teaspoon honey

⅛ teaspoon salt

¼ teaspoon freshly ground black pepper

¾ PLATE

PREP TIME:
10 minutes

COOK TIME:
15 minutes

PER SERVING:
Calories: 332
Total fat: 27g
Saturated fat: 4g
Cholesterol: 98mg
Sodium: 343mg
Carbs: 7g
Fiber: 3g
Sugars: 2g
Protein: 17g

TO MAKE THE SALAD

1. In a large skillet, cook the turkey bacon over medium heat until crisp. Transfer to paper towels to drain. Break into bite-size pieces.

2. Drain off all but 1 teaspoon of bacon fat from the skillet. Season the chicken breasts lightly with the salt and pepper. Cook the chicken in the bacon fat over medium-high heat, turning once, until the juices run clear, 7 to 10 minutes. Remove from the pan, let cool, and cut into strips.

3. Arrange the spinach and lettuce on a large platter. Top with the chicken strips, avocado, bacon, hardboiled eggs, cucumber, and cherry tomatoes.

TO MAKE THE DRESSING

In a small bowl, whisk together the olive oil, vinegar, mustard, honey, salt, and pepper. Drizzle over the salad and serve.

Complete the Plate: Serve this with an additional starch/grain dish such as Sweet Potato Fries (page 167) or Macaroni and Cheese with Mixed Vegetables (page 178).

Southwestern Stuffed Peppers with Turkey, Corn, and Black Beans

FULL PLATE

PREP TIME:
15 minutes

COOK TIME:
25 minutes

PER SERVING:
Calories: 284
Total fat: 10g
Saturated fat: 3g
Cholesterol: 61mg
Sodium: 211mg
Carbs: 30g
Fiber: 6g
Sugars: 4g
Protein: 21g

SERVES 6 (1 PEPPER EACH) If you are looking for a simple weeknight meal to prepare, this is it! Even after a busy day, you can make these stuffed peppers with minimal effort yet make enough to take leftovers for lunch the next day. I have even been known to freeze extra so that I always have a healthy meal on hand. These stuffed peppers are a no-fuss and flavorful way to complete your entire plate in one dish—now that's what I call easy!

6 green, yellow, or red bell peppers

1 teaspoon extra-virgin olive oil

1 pound lean ground turkey

2 large tomatoes, diced

¾ cup cooked or canned black beans, rinsed and drained

½ cup frozen (thawed) yellow corn

2 garlic cloves, minced

1 teaspoon onion powder

1 teaspoon chipotle chile powder

1 cup cooked brown rice

¼ cup shredded sharp Cheddar cheese

1. Preheat the oven to 350ºF.

2. Bring a large pot of water to a boil over medium-high heat. Slice off the tops of the bell peppers and clean out the insides. Add the bell peppers to the boiling water and cook for 10 minutes. Drain the bell peppers and place in an 8-by-11-inch baking dish.

3. While the peppers are cooking, heat the olive oil in a large skillet over medium-high heat. Add the turkey and cook, crumbling the meat with a spoon or spatula, until brown, 7 to 8 minutes.

4. Add the tomatoes, cover, and reduce the heat to medium. Cook until the tomatoes are broken down, 2 to 3 minutes.

5. Add the black beans, corn, garlic, onion powder, and chipotle chile powder. Stir and cook until the beans and corn are warmed through, 1 to 2 minutes. Stir in the brown rice and remove from the heat.

6. Stuff each bell pepper with the turkey mixture. Sprinkle 2 teaspoons of Cheddar cheese on top of each stuffed bell pepper. Bake for 15 minutes.

Tip: Bell peppers are my absolute favorite vegetable! Bell peppers start out green and then the longer they are left on the plant, they turn yellow, orange, and finally red. While all bell peppers boast nutritional benefits, red ones contain significantly more vitamin C than green ones.

Old-Fashioned Turkey Meatloaf with Sweet Tomato Sauce

½ PLATE

PREP TIME:
15 minutes

COOK TIME:
30 minutes

PER SERVING:
Calories: 287
Total fat: 18g
Saturated fat: 3g
Cholesterol:
136mg
Sodium: 288mg
Carbs: 20g
Fiber: 3g
Sugars: 7g
Protein: 26g

SERVES 4 (1 SLICE EACH) Meatloaf is a staple in my family. This recipe was originally given to me by my brother, who enjoys meatloaf almost every week! What I love about meatloaf is that you can make it your own. In this recipe, feel free to adjust the spices, add extra onions, or change the veggies to include your personal favorites.

FOR THE MEATLOAF

Nonstick cooking spray

1 pound lean ground turkey breast

2 scallions, chopped (green and white parts)

½ cup diced red bell pepper

½ cup chopped onion

1 large egg, beaten

2 garlic cloves, minced

¼ cup whole-wheat bread crumbs

¼ cup oat flour (make your own by pulsing rolled oats in a food processor)

1 teaspoon dried Italian herb blend

¼ teaspoon onion powder

¼ teaspoon freshly ground black pepper

¼ teaspoon salt

Pinch cayenne pepper

FOR THE SWEET TOMATO SAUCE

1 medium tomato, sliced

1 date, pitted

2 teaspoons Worcestershire sauce

1 teaspoon chili powder

1. Preheat the oven to 350°F. Lightly coat an 8-inch square baking dish with nonstick cooking spray.

2. Combine all the meatloaf ingredients in a large mixing bowl. Mix well with your hands until the ingredients are well combined. Press the meatloaf mixture into the prepared baking dish and bake until a thermometer inserted in the middle reads 160°F, 25 to 30 minutes.

eat what you love DIABETES COOKBOOK

3. While the meatloaf is cooking, combine the tomato, date, Worcestershire sauce, and chili powder in a food processor and blend until smooth.

4. Transfer the tomato mixture to a saucepan and cook over medium heat until it becomes slightly thickened (the consistency of a smoothie), 10 to 12 minutes.

5. Spread the tomato mixture over the meatloaf for the last 5 to 10 minutes of cooking time. Remove from the oven and cut into 4 slices. Serve.

Tip: Garlic contains a powerful plant nutrient called allyl sulfide, which may help lower cholesterol as well as fight cancer and heart disease. To get the maximum benefits, mince your garlic about 15 minutes prior to cooking to let the allyl sulfides fully evolve.

Complete the Plate: Serve with your favorite vegetable side and a starch/grain side, if more carbs are desired. I love to serve Five Minute Brussels Sprouts and Almonds (page 154) with this meal, along with Old-Fashioned Sweet Potato Bake with Pecans (page 166).

Steak Fajitas with Avocado Salad

Beef and Pork Mains

No book that highlights comfort foods would be complete without a few delicious beef and pork dishes. While these should not be eaten on a daily basis, they can certainly be enjoyed as a part of your balanced plate that includes high-fiber grains and nourishing vegetables.

In this chapter, you will find ways to savor the healthiest cuts of beef and pork. I have included here all my favorite recipes for traditional comfort-food meat dishes, ensuring they are satisfying, filling, and diabetes-friendly, all at the same time. Perhaps most important, be assured that they don't lack in comforting flavor—these recipes are sure to be enjoyed by all!

Beef and Bean Chili

SERVES 8 (1½ CUPS EACH) This chili is loaded with beans, making it a filling and fiber-rich meal. Chipotle chile powder delivers a fragrant bite, while the trio of beans gives it a lovely appearance in the bowl and great texture. Like most chilis and stews, this one tastes even better after a period of rest. Make it a day or two in advance, then refrigerate it to allow the flavors to really meld.

1 tablespoon extra-virgin olive oil

1 onion, diced

1 bell pepper, seeded and diced

2 teaspoons ground cumin

1 pound extra-lean ground beef

1 (28-ounce) can crushed tomatoes

2 cups water

1 teaspoon chipotle chile powder

2 teaspoons chili powder

1 (15-ounce) can black beans, drained and rinsed

1 (15-ounce) can pinto beans, drained and rinsed

1 (15-ounce) can kidney beans, drained and rinsed

¼ teaspoon freshly ground black pepper

FULL PLATE

PREP TIME:
10 minutes

COOK TIME:
1 hour

PER SERVING:
Calories: 288
Total fat: 6g
Saturated fat: 2g
Cholesterol: 35mg
Sodium: 346mg
Carbs: 37g
Fiber: 11g
Sugars: 7g
Protein: 24g

1. In a large Dutch oven, heat the olive oil over medium-high heat. Add the onion and bell pepper and sauté until softened. Add the cumin and cook until fragrant, about another minute.

2. Add the ground beef and cook, breaking apart the meat with a spatula, until no longer pink.

3. Add the tomatoes, water, chipotle chile powder, and chili powder. Bring to a boil, reduce the heat, and simmer for 30 minutes.

4. Add the beans and pepper and continue to simmer for 20 minutes. Serve hot.

Complete the Plate: You can always add more vegetables, so if you are feeling hungry, consider adding a Simple Green Salad with Garlic, Lemon, and Olive Oil Vinaigrette (page 145) or Summer Strawberry-Arugula Salad (page 141).

Spaghetti Squash Lasagna Bowls

FULL PLATE

PREP TIME:
10 minutes

COOK TIME:
1 hour

PER SERVING:
Calories: 379
Total fat: 14g
Saturated fat: 7g
Cholesterol: 99mg
Sodium: 689mg
Carbs: 27g
Fiber: 6g
Sugars: 11g
Protein: 38g

SERVES 4 (1 SQUASH LASAGNA EACH) When cooked, spaghetti squash transforms from a solid, hard vegetable into pliable strings similar to angel hair pasta. This amazing change gives way to its unique ability to double as a tasty pasta substitute perfect for a marinara-based preparation. Use the squash halves as bowls, and you have a simple, self-contained meal that provides a unique and delicious stand-in for traditional noodle-based lasagna.

2 small spaghetti squash	¼ teaspoon salt
8 ounces extra-lean ground beef	¼ teaspoon freshly ground black pepper
1 small onion, diced	½ cup reduced-fat ricotta cheese
1 (15-ounce) can diced tomatoes, drained	½ cup shredded mozzarella cheese

1. Preheat the oven to 350ºF.

2. Carefully cut each spaghetti squash lengthwise and remove any seeds with a spoon. Place the squash halves cut-side down in a large baking pan and pour in about ½ inch of water. Cook until the squash can easily be pierced, 30 to 45 minutes.

3. Remove the squash from the oven, let cool for 10 minutes, and use a fork to remove and reserve the flesh, leaving about ¼ inch of flesh attached to each shell. Arrange the shells cut-side up on the baking dish.

4. In a skillet, brown the ground beef over medium-high heat. Add the diced onion and continue cooking, stirring regularly, until it becomes translucent. Add the tomatoes, salt, and pepper and stir to combine. Continue cooking until heated through.

eat what you love DIABETES COOKBOOK

5. Fold in the reserved squash flesh and remove the pan from the heat. Fold the ricotta cheese into the mixture.

6. Pack each squash shell with one quarter of the meat and squash mixture, packing it firmly as you go. Add 2 tablespoons of mozzarella cheese to the top of each squash.

7. Return the baking dish to the oven and bake until the cheese is melted and browned on top, 5 to 6 minutes.

Tip: In anticipation of a busy night, prepare the entire recipe through step 6 the day before, then refrigerate, covered, until ready to cook. Bake the squash at 350ºF until heated through and the cheese is browned, about 30 minutes.

Complete the Plate: You can always add more vegetables, so if you are feeling hungry, consider adding a Simple Green Salad with Garlic, Lemon, and Olive Oil Vinaigrette (page 145) or Sweet and Tender Kale Salad (page 143).

Zoodles with Marinara and Meatballs

FULL PLATE

PREP TIME:
20 minutes

COOK TIME:
25 minutes

PER SERVING:
Calories: 341
Total fat: 18g
Saturated fat: 4g
Cholesterol: 87mg
Sodium: 633mg
Carbs: 29g
Fiber: 7g
Sugars: 16g
Protein: 21g

SERVES 4 (2 CUPS ZOODLES + 3 MEATBALLS EACH) These meatballs have all the beefy flavor we love, but they pack in some added nutrient density with the addition of quinoa and carrots. Not only are they delicious and versatile, they can stretch your food budget, too! Here they are served on a bed of zoodles, or zucchini noodles, a super low-carb way to get your pasta fix. Be sure to use medium-size zucchini, but not large ones, which have large, hardened seeds and a limp texture.

FOR THE MEATBALLS

8 ounces lean ground beef

½ cup cooked quinoa

2 tablespoons finely chopped onion

¼ cup grated carrot

1 garlic clove, minced

½ teaspoon freshly ground black pepper

1 large egg, lightly beaten

FOR THE MARINARA

2 tablespoons extra-virgin olive oil

2 garlic cloves, minced

1 (28-ounce) can crushed tomatoes

1 teaspoon honey

½ teaspoon salt

Pinch freshly ground black pepper

FOR THE ZOODLES

4 medium zucchini

2 tablespoons extra-virgin olive oil, divided

TO MAKE THE MEATBALLS

1. Preheat the oven to 450ºF. Line a baking sheet with parchment paper and set aside.

2. In a large bowl, combine all the ingredients and mix well. Using your hands, shape the meat into 12 small, firmly packed balls, and transfer them to the lined baking sheet.

3. Bake until cooked through and browned, about 15 minutes.

eat what you love DIABETES COOKBOOK

TO MAKE THE MARINARA

1. While the meatballs are in the oven, heat the olive oil in a small pot over medium heat. Add the garlic and sauté for 1 minute, until it just begins to turn golden brown.

2. Add the tomatoes, honey, salt, and pepper and stir to combine. Simmer for about 10 minutes to let the flavors combine.

TO MAKE THE ZOODLES

1. Using a spiralizer, cut the zucchini into noodles 4 to 6 inches long.

2. Heat 1 tablespoon of olive oil over medium-high heat. Add half of the zoodles. Using tongs, stir the zoodles around the pan. Continue to stir until the zoodles become slightly tender, about 2 minutes total. Transfer to a bowl. Repeat with the remaining zoodles and oil.

3. Divide the zoodles among four plates and top each with 3 meatballs and some marinara.

Beef and Mushroom Sliders with Brie

½ PLATE

PREP TIME:
10 minutes

COOK TIME:
15 minutes

PER SERVING:
Calories: 325
Total fat: 16g
Saturated fat: 7g
Cholesterol:
113mg
Sodium: 379mg
Carbs: 20g
Fiber: 4g
Sugars: 3g
Protein: 27g

SERVES 4 (1 SLIDER EACH) Mushrooms add considerable heft and enable you to enjoy a nutrient-dense burger while cutting some serious fat. Cremini mushrooms are ideal for this burger, as their mild flavor blends well with the beef, forming a firm patty that contains half the meat but all the flavor. Choose extra-lean ground beef for the most heart-healthy option.

12 ounces cremini mushrooms

2 teaspoons organic canola oil

¼ teaspoon salt

¼ teaspoon freshly ground black pepper

8 ounces extra-lean ground beef

¼ cup chopped onion

1 large egg, beaten

4 whole-wheat rolls, cut in half

4 slices Brie cheese

1. In a food processor, pulse the mushrooms until they are coarsely ground.

2. In a large skillet, heat the oil over medium-high heat. Add the mushrooms, salt, and pepper and cook, stirring frequently, until the mushrooms brown and the juices evaporate. Remove from the heat and allow to cool for 10 minutes.

3. In a mixing bowl, combine the mushrooms, beef, onion, and egg. Form into 4 patties, pressing firmly so they hold together.

4. Heat a large skillet over medium-high heat. Add the burgers and cook for 4 to 5 minutes per side. Place the burgers on the buns, top with cheese, and serve.

Complete the Plate: While this dish has a serving of mushrooms, I encourage you to add an additional serving of vegetables. Serve with a Simple Green Salad with Garlic, Lemon, and Olive Oil Vinaigrette (page 145), Fermented Dill Pickles (page 148), or Classic Creamy Picnic Coleslaw (page 146).

Thai-Style Beef Curry

FULL PLATE

PREP TIME:
20 minutes

COOK TIME:
10 minutes

PER SERVING:
Calories: 351
Total fat: 15g
Saturated fat: 8g
Cholesterol: 71mg
Sodium: 751mg
Carbs: 22g
Fiber: 6g
Sugars: 5g
Protein: 30g

SERVES 4 (1 CUP EACH) This healthy take on Thai comfort food—a classic red curry—will leave your appetite satiated and your taste buds fulfilled. Make the paste yourself using fresh ingredients, or substitute a store-bought red curry paste if you are in a hurry. Use light coconut milk to cut back on fat, and visit an Asian store for ingredients like shrimp paste and fresh lemongrass to set you on your way.

FOR THE CURRY PASTE

1 shallot

1 stalk lemongrass, outer layer and woody upper area discarded, cut into 1-inch sections

1 Thai red chile, stemmed and seeded

4 garlic cloves, peeled

2-inch knob ginger, peeled and sliced

2 tablespoons freshly squeezed lime juice

1 tablespoon fish sauce

1 teaspoon shrimp paste

1 teaspoon ground cumin

1 teaspoon ground coriander

¼ teaspoon ground white pepper

FOR THE CURRY

1 (14-ounce) can light coconut milk, divided

1 pound flank steak, thinly sliced against the grain

3 garlic cloves, minced

1 teaspoon grated fresh ginger

½ medium onion, diced

1 red bell pepper, seeded and sliced

1 head broccoli, broken into florets

2 teaspoons fish sauce, plus more if desired

1 teaspoon sugar (optional)

¼ cup chopped fresh cilantro

eat what you love DIABETES COOKBOOK

TO MAKE THE CURRY PASTE

Combine all the ingredients in a food processor. Pulse until coarsely ground. Add a tablespoon or two of water and continue pulsing to form a smooth paste.

TO MAKE THE CURRY

1. Heat a large wok over medium-high heat. Transfer the curry paste to the wok, along with 2 to 3 tablespoons of the coconut milk. Cook, stirring constantly, until fragrant, about 1 minute.

2. Add the flank steak and cook, stirring constantly, until it is well browned. Use a spatula to push the steak to the side of the wok, away from the direct heat. Add the garlic and ginger and stir-fry until fragrant. Add the onion, bell pepper, and broccoli and stir to mix. Push the steak back into the middle of the wok and add the remaining coconut milk.

3. Bring the liquid to a simmer and continue to cook until the vegetables are fork-tender, about 10 minutes. Remove from the heat and stir in the fish sauce. Taste and adjust the seasoning, adding the sugar (if using) and more fish sauce according to your preference. Garnish with the cilantro.

Tip: If you choose to use a premade curry paste, start with just 1 tablespoon of the paste and, if desired, add more later on. Commercially prepared curry pastes are typically much hotter than this one, so you'll need less for this recipe.

Complete the Plate: While this recipe does contain some carbs, feel free to serve over ⅓ cup of brown rice if more carbs are needed or desired.

Steak Fajitas with Avocado Salad

SERVES 8 (1 FAJITA EACH) In this healthier version of fajitas, a generous serving of avocado salad is paired with a few juicy slices of marinated lean flank steak. This winning combination provides a great dose of heart-healthy monounsaturated fats while still embodying the flavor and feel of a classic fajita dinner.

FULL PLATE

PREP TIME:
15 minutes +
1 hour to marinate

COOK TIME:
15 minutes

PER SERVING:
Calories: 388
Total fat: 21g
Saturated fat: 4g
Cholesterol: 44mg
Sodium: 525mg
Carbs: 34g
Fiber: 7g
Sugars: 3g
Protein: 21g

FOR THE FLANK STEAK

Juice of 3 limes

2 tablespoons extra-virgin olive oil

1 teaspoon ground cumin

1 jalapeño, seeded and roughly chopped

¼ cup chopped fresh cilantro leaves and stems

1 (1¼-pound) flank steak

1 teaspoon organic canola oil

FOR THE AVOCADO SALAD

2 tablespoons extra-virgin olive oil

2 tablespoons freshly squeezed lemon juice

½ teaspoon salt

¼ teaspoon freshly ground black pepper

2 tablespoons chopped fresh cilantro leaves

2 ripe avocados, pitted, peeled, and thinly sliced

1 bunch red radishes, thinly sliced

FOR THE FAJITAS

8 whole-wheat flour tortillas

Fresh cilantro leaves, for garnish

2 limes, cut into wedges, for garnish

eat what you love DIABETES COOKBOOK

TO MAKE THE FLANK STEAK

1. In a large bowl, combine the lime juice, olive oil, cumin, jalapeño, and cilantro. Mix well. Add the steak and flip it so that the meat is coated all over in the marinade. Cover and refrigerate for at least 1 hour or up to 10 hours.

2. Remove the steak from the marinade, shaking off any excess. Heat a cast-iron pan over medium-high heat for 2 minutes. Add the canola oil. When the oil is hot, cook the steak for 3 to 5 minutes per side, depending on desired doneness (3 minutes will yield a medium-rare steak, while 5 will yield a medium to well-done steak). Transfer the steak to a plate and tent with aluminum foil for 5 minutes. Slice the steak thinly against the grain.

TO MAKE THE AVOCADO SALAD

In a mixing bowl, whisk together the olive oil, lemon juice, salt, and pepper. Add the cilantro, avocados, and radishes and toss to coat.

TO ASSEMBLE THE FAJITAS

Arrange a scoop of the avocado salad on each tortilla and top with a few slices of steak. Garnish with the cilantro and lime wedges and serve.

Complete the Plate: While this dish creates a complete plate, you can always eat more vegetables. Feel free to add leafy greens to your avocado salad or onions or bell peppers to your fajitas.

Marinated Flank Steak on a Bed of Greens

SERVES 4 (2 CUPS GREENS + 4 OUNCES STEAK EACH) Enjoy the home-style goodness of steak on a bed of greens in this savory dish. Marinated in an unexpected yet flavor-boosting blend of coffee, balsamic vinegar, and fish sauce, this steak pops with flavor. Slice it thinly when cooked to your liking, and serve it over microgreens for a nutrient-packed meal that will satisfy your craving for red meat comfort-food classics.

¾ PLATE

PREP TIME:
15 minutes +
30 minutes to marinate

COOK TIME:
10 minutes

PER SERVING:
Calories: 260
Total fat: 14g
Saturated fat: 3g
Cholesterol: 70mg
Sodium: 607mg
Carbs: 6g
Fiber: 1g
Sugars: 3g
Protein: 26g

FOR THE STEAK

¼ cup balsamic vinegar

2 teaspoons extra-virgin olive oil

1 tablespoon fish sauce

1 tablespoon finely ground coffee

2 garlic cloves, minced

½ teaspoon freshly ground black pepper

1 (1-pound) flank steak

FOR THE GREENS

1½ tablespoons extra-virgin olive oil

2 tablespoons red wine vinegar

1 teaspoon Dijon mustard

1 garlic clove, minced

¼ teaspoon salt

¼ teaspoon freshly ground black pepper

8 cups packed microgreens or baby greens (arugula, spinach, chard, beetroot)

TO MAKE THE STEAK

1. In a large bowl, whisk together the vinegar, olive oil, fish sauce, coffee, garlic, and black pepper. Add the steak and flip it so that the meat is coated all over in the marinade. Cover and marinate for 30 minutes to 1 hour.

2. Preheat the broiler on high.

3. Remove the steak from the marinade, shaking off any excess. Put the steak on a roasting rack over a pan and place it under the broiler. Broil, flipping once, until cooked to your liking, 8 to 10 minutes, or longer if desired. Let the steak sit for 10 minutes before slicing against the grain into thin strips. ▶

TO MAKE THE GREENS

1. In a small bowl, whisk together the olive oil, vinegar, mustard, garlic, salt, and pepper.

2. Put the microgreens in a large bowl. Pour the vinaigrette over the greens and toss to combine. Arrange some of the greens on each plate, top with sliced steak, and serve.

Complete the Plate: This goes great with Sweet Potato Fries (page 167).

Old-Fashioned Beef Stew with Rutabaga and Turnips

SERVES 6 (1½ CUPS EACH) On a cold night there is nothing as comforting as a bowl of warm beef stew. Filling and flavorful, this stew is laden with juicy pieces of beef, while the classic potatoes are replaced with rutabagas and turnips for a high-flavor, lower-carb dish.

1 pound eye of round or bottom round roast

1 large onion, chopped

4 celery stalks, chopped

4 cups water or low-sodium beef or chicken broth

1 (14.5-ounce) can low-sodium diced tomatoes, drained

2 bay leaves

1 teaspoon dried oregano

1 teaspoon dried thyme

1 teaspoon salt

½ teaspoon black pepper

2 cups diced peeled rutabaga

1 cup diced peeled turnip

1 medium carrot, peeled and diced

FULL PLATE

PREP TIME:
10 minutes

COOK TIME:
1 hour 30 minutes

PER SERVING:
Calories: 203
Total fat: 5g
Saturated fat: 2g
Cholesterol: 58mg
Sodium: 563mg
Carbs: 15g
Fiber: 4g
Sugars: 8g
Protein: 24g

1. Heat a large Dutch oven over medium-high heat. Add the beef to the pot and sear each side until well browned.

2. Add the onion and celery to the pot and sauté until they begin to soften. Add the water, tomatoes, bay leaves, oregano, thyme, salt, and pepper and bring to a boil. Reduce the heat, cover, and simmer for 45 minutes.

3. Add the rutabaga, turnip, and carrot. Cook until the vegetables are tender and the beef breaks apart easily, about 40 minutes.

4. Turn off the heat and let the stew sit for 10 minutes. Using a large spoon, skim the layer of fat from the top of the stew and discard. Serve hot.

Tip: To make this in a slow cooker, brown the meat in a skillet and then transfer it to the slow cooker, along with all the other ingredients. Cover and cook for 6 to 8 hours on low.

Complete the Plate: This recipe can use an additional serving of vegetables and starch/grains, so I love to add the Quinoa and Vegetable Pilau (page 175) to satisfy both needs.

Sweet-and-Sour Pork and Veggie Stir-Fry

FULL PLATE

PREP TIME:
10 minutes +
30 minutes to
marinate

COOK TIME:
10 minutes

PER SERVING:
Calories: 264
Total fat: 11g
Saturated fat: 2g
Cholesterol: 54mg
Sodium: 603mg
Carbs: 18g
Fiber: 2g
Sugars: 12g
Protein: 22g

SERVES 5 (1 CUP EACH) This quick and easy stir-fry is lower in fat, sugar, and salt than the one you may get at your local restaurant, but it shines with flavor nonetheless. Be sure to cut the pork loin when it is slightly frozen—this will allow you to get the thinnest cuts; if you are using a fresh pork loin, simply place it in the freezer for 30 minutes before slicing.

FOR THE PORK

2 tablespoons rice wine or sake

½ teaspoon salt

1 tablespoon cornstarch

1 pound pork loin, sliced ⅛ inch thick (see headnote)

1 tablespoon organic canola oil

FOR THE STIR-FRY

½ cup canned pineapple chunks

¼ cup canned pineapple juice

3 tablespoons rice vinegar

1 teaspoon toasted sesame oil

1 teaspoon cornstarch

2 teaspoons organic canola oil

1 red bell pepper, seeded and sliced

1 green bell pepper, seeded and sliced

1 onion, sliced

10 ounces button mushrooms, sliced

TO MAKE THE PORK

1. In a large bowl, mix the rice wine, salt, and cornstarch. Add the pork loin and toss to combine. Set aside for 30 minutes.

2. In a large wok, heat the canola oil over medium-high heat. In batches, pan-fry the pork slices until just starting to brown, about 1 minute per side. (They will not be cooked through.) Use a slotted spoon to transfer the pork to a plate. Repeat with the remaining pork. Wipe the wok clean with a paper towel.

TO MAKE THE STIR-FRY

1. In a small bowl, combine the pineapple chunks, juice, vinegar, sesame oil, and cornstarch. Set aside.

2. Heat the canola oil in the wok over medium-high heat. Add the red and green peppers and onion to the pan. Cook for 1 minute, stirring constantly. Add the mushrooms and cook for 1 additional minute. Return the pork to the wok and continue to cook until brown spots begin to appear on the meat, 1 to 2 minutes.

3. Using a spatula, push all the meat and vegetables to the sides of the wok. Add the pineapple mixture to the center and bring to a boil. Cook until the sauce begins to thicken, about 1 minute. Stir the meat and vegetables into the sauce to coat. Serve.

Tip: The marinating and cooking step used in this recipe is called velveting. This technique is commonly used in Chinese cooking to both lock in flavor and give the meat a soft, tender texture.

Complete the Plate: While this recipe already contains one serving of carbohydrates, consider adding 1/3 to 2/3 cup of brown rice or another whole grain if you would like to increase the amount of carbs in your meal.

Apple-Cinnamon Slow Cooker Pork Loin

½ PLATE

PREP TIME:
10 minutes

COOK TIME:
6 hours

PER SERVING:
Calories: 251
Total fat: 6g
Saturated fat: 2g
Cholesterol: 98mg
Sodium: 277mg
Carbs: 17g
Fiber: 4g
Sugars: 11g
Protein: 33g

SERVES 8 (½ CUP EACH) The classic flavors of apple and cinnamon come together wonderfully with pork. While the flavors may not seem like a natural match, this home-style combination evokes memories of cool fall nights, and plays with the blend of sweet and savory so well. Cinnamon delivers big flavor, allowing you to cut back on salt without anyone noticing the difference.

1 (2-pound) pork tenderloin

½ teaspoon salt

½ teaspoon freshly ground black pepper

3 teaspoons ground cinnamon, divided

1 tablespoon organic canola oil

2 onions, cut into 6 wedges each

3 firm, sweet apples (such as Honeycrisp or Fuji), cored and cut into wedges

¼ cup water

1. Cut 8 to 10 slits about 1 inch deep on one side of the pork tenderloin. Sprinkle the sides of the tenderloin with the salt, pepper, and 1 teaspoon of cinnamon.

2. In a large skillet, heat the oil over medium-high heat. Brown the tenderloin on all sides.

3. Cover the bottom of the slow cooker with the onion wedges and a few apple wedges. Sprinkle them with the remaining 2 teaspoons of cinnamon. Pour in the water. Place the tenderloin on top of the onions and apples and stuff the remaining apples into the slits of the pork. Cover and cook on low for 6 hours. Slice the pork and serve with the onions and apples.

Tip: For easy cleanup when using a slow cooker, buy slow cooker inserts, which line the cooker before cooking. This way, when you are done, you can simply throw the insert away and the appliance can be wiped clean, ready for the next use.

Complete the Plate: Pair with a starchy side such as Macaroni and Cheese with Mixed Vegetables (page 178), Roasted Broccoli and Parmesan Millet Bake (page 176), or Mashed Cauliflower and Potatoes (page 170), and a vegetable side such as Simple Green Salad with Garlic, Lemon, and Olive Oil Vinaigrette (page 145) or Sautéed Garlic, Ginger, and Shallot Green Beans (page 156).

Slow Cooker Pulled-Pork Sandwich

SERVES 8 (1 SANDWICH EACH) A slow cooker makes mealtime a breeze, and in the case of this pulled pork sandwich recipe, it's also a great way to have your house smelling amazing! Pulled-pork sandwiches are the perfect pairing with Classic Creamy Picnic Coleslaw (page 146), which, if you are in the mood, can be heaped right onto your sandwich to complement the meat with a firm and flavorful crunch.

½ PLATE

PREP TIME:
10 minutes

COOK TIME:
4 to 5 hours

PER SERVING:
Calories: 296
Total fat: 4g
Saturated fat: 1g
Cholesterol: 74mg
Sodium: 620mg
Carbs: 36g
Fiber: 5g
Sugars: 8g
Protein: 30g

1 (2-pound) pork tenderloin

½ cup ketchup

3 tablespoons tomato paste

2 tablespoons cider vinegar

2 tablespoons Worcestershire sauce

1 tablespoon pure maple syrup

1 tablespoon brown mustard

8 whole-wheat sandwich rolls

1. Place the pork tenderloin in the slow cooker.

2. In a small bowl, whisk together the ketchup, tomato paste, vinegar, Worcestershire, maple syrup, and mustard. Pour the mixture over the pork.

3. Cover and cook the pork on low for 4 to 5 hours. Using two forks, shred the meat and mix it back into the sauce.

4. Serve the pulled pork on the sandwich rolls.

Complete the Plate: Serve with a vegetable side such as Sweet and Tender Kale Salad (page 143), Classic Creamy Picnic Coleslaw (page 146), or Five-Minute Brussels Sprouts and Almonds (page 154). Add Fermented Dill Pickles (page 148) for an extra serving of veggies.

Shrimp Zoodle Scampi

Seafood Mains

While fish may not always be the first food that comes to mind when you think "comfort food," it certainly deserves a place at your table. In this chapter you will find a variety of seafood choices that are all great sources of lean protein. I think you will be pleasantly surprised to see the range of dishes represented here, each with its own nourishing elements.

According to the American Heart Association, we should all be consuming fish at least two times per week since fish, especially those high in omega-3 fats, can help prevent heart disease.

My hope is that you will find quick and easy recipes here that you can begin using on a regular basis, and that, if you aren't already, you will find yourself enjoying and looking forward to your seafood meals.

Cashew and Parmesan Crusted Salmon

SERVES 4 (1 FILLET EACH) The nutritional benefits of salmon are hard to beat! The omega-3 fatty acids contained in salmon are considered essential: since our body cannot produce them, we must obtain them from the food we eat. Omega-3 fats may help reduce the chances of heart disease, which is especially important since individuals with diabetes have an increased risk of heart disease.

¼ PLATE

PREP TIME:
5 minutes

COOK TIME:
15 minutes

PER SERVING:
Calories: 392
Total fat: 24g
Saturated fat: 5g
Cholesterol: 99mg
Sodium: 175mg
Carbohydrates: 5g
Sugars: 1g
Fiber: 0g
Protein: 39g

Nonstick cooking spray

4 (4- to 6-ounce) wild salmon fillets

4 teaspoons extra-virgin olive oil

¼ cup unsalted cashews

¼ cup fresh parsley leaves

¼ cup grated Parmesan cheese

2 garlic cloves, peeled

¼ teaspoon freshly ground black pepper

4 lemon wedges

1. Preheat the oven to 350°F. Line a baking sheet with aluminum foil and lightly coat the foil with nonstick cooking spray.

2. Rinse the salmon fillets, pat them dry with paper towels, and place skin-side down on the prepared baking sheet. Brush each salmon fillet with 1 teaspoon of olive oil.

3. Combine the cashews, parsley, Parmesan cheese, garlic, and pepper in a food processor. Pulse 20 to 30 times to yield a fine mixture. Spread the mixture evenly over the fillets.

4. Bake for 12 to 13 minutes. Then turn the broiler on high and broil until the topping is lightly browned, about 2 more minutes.

5. Transfer the fillets to serving plates and squeeze the juice of a lemon wedge over each.

Complete the Plate: Serve with your favorite vegetable side and starch/grain side. I suggest adding Simple Green Salad with Garlic, Lemon, and Olive Oil Vinaigrette (page 145) and Wild Rice Pilaf with Broccoli and Carrots (page 173).

Miso Salmon

SERVES 4 (1 FILLET EACH) Salmon is a firm, fatty fish and a comfort-food classic. Miso, a long-fermented paste made from soybeans, is a Japanese condiment that makes its way into many of its country's notable dishes. In this simple preparation, miso glazes the salmon and imparts a salty, flavorful finish.

¼ PLATE

PREP TIME:
10 minutes +
30 minutes to
marinate

COOK TIME:
10 minutes

PER SERVING:
Calories: 278
Total fat: 12g
Saturated fat: 2g
Cholesterol: 94mg
Sodium: 537mg
Carbs: 6g
Fiber: 0g
Sugars: 3g
Protein: 35g

2 tablespoons red or white miso

2 tablespoons mirin

1 tablespoon sake

1 tablespoon low-sodium soy sauce

¼ teaspoon toasted sesame oil

4 (4- to 6-ounce) salmon fillets

1. In a large shallow bowl or baking dish, whisk together the miso, mirin, sake, soy sauce, and sesame oil. Add the salmon fillets to the marinade, skin-side up. Cover and refrigerate for 30 minutes.

2. Preheat the broiler on high. Line a baking sheet with parchment paper.

3. Transfer the salmon to the lined baking sheet. Broil until the fish flakes easily, 10 to 12 minutes.

Tip: Find miso at many well-stocked grocery stores, Asian markets, or health food stores. Typically sold in 1-pound packages, this versatile condiment can be stored for up to 1 year in your refrigerator.

Complete the Plate: Pair with Old-Fashioned Sweet Potato Bake with Pecans (page 166), or ⅔ cup of brown rice and a Simple Green Salad with Garlic, Lemon, and Olive Oil Vinaigrette (page 145) or Sweet and Tender Kale Salad (page 143).

Cinnamon-Citrus Cod

SERVES 2 (1 FILLET EACH) I love quick and tasty recipes that can be added easily to any meal. This cod recipe is carb-free, so it serves as the protein in your balanced plate. The simple and unique flavor combination of cinnamon and lemon juice can be paired with your favorite vegetable dish and starchy side.

Nonstick cooking spray

2 (4- to 6-ounce) cod fillets

2 teaspoons extra-virgin olive oil

1 tablespoon freshly squeezed lemon juice

⅛ teaspoon salt

⅛ teaspoon freshly ground black pepper

½ teaspoon ground cinnamon

½ teaspoon ground cumin

¼ teaspoon fresh, grated ginger

¼ teaspoon garlic powder

¼ PLATE

PREP TIME:
5 minutes

COOK TIME:
10 minutes

PER SERVING:
Calories: 186
Total fat: 6g
Saturated fat: 1g
Cholesterol: 73mg
Sodium: 238mg
Carbs: 1g
Fiber: 0g
Sugars: 0g
Protein 30g

1. Preheat the oven to 400°F. Lightly coat a baking sheet with nonstick cooking spray.

2. Place the cod on the prepared baking sheet and drizzle each fillet with olive oil and lemon juice. Season each with the salt and pepper.

3. In a small mixing bowl, combine the cinnamon, cumin, ginger, and garlic powder. Sprinkle evenly over the cod fillets.

4. Bake until the fish flakes easily, 10 to 12 minutes.

Complete the Plate: Serve with your favorite vegetable side and starch/grain side. My choices are Grilled Zucchini Salad (page 157) and Crispy Sage-Roasted Root Vegetables (page 165).

Fish Tacos

FULL PLATE

PREP TIME:
10 minutes +
15 minutes to
marinate

COOK TIME:
5 minutes

PER SERVING:
Calories: 304
Total fat: 10g
Saturated fat: 2g
Cholesterol: 56mg
Sodium: 256mg
Carbs: 29g
Fiber: 5g
Sugars: 4g
Protein: 25g

SERVES 4 (2 TACOS EACH) Halibut is a mildly flavored, firm white fish that is perfectly suited to tacos, absorbing as it does the bright flavor of the cilantro and lime marinade. Served on a corn tortilla and topped with a spicy salsa verde, this is a simple and delicious dish that just screams of summer. Toss the salsa together while the fish marinates, and you'll be enjoying these tacos in just 30 minutes.

FOR THE SALSA

8 ounces tomatillos, husked

2 garlic cloves, peeled

2 serrano chiles, seeded

½ cup packed fresh cilantro leaves

¼ cup water

¼ teaspoon salt

FOR THE TACOS

Grated zest and juice of 1 lime

2 garlic cloves, peeled

1 bunch cilantro, leaves and stems coarsely chopped

1 bunch scallions, coarsely chopped (green and white parts)

1 teaspoon ground cumin

2 tablespoons extra-virgin olive oil, divided

1 pound halibut

8 small corn tortillas

eat what you love DIABETES COOKBOOK

TO MAKE THE SALSA

Combine all the ingredients in a blender. Pulse until chunky.

TO MAKE THE TACOS

1. Combine the lime zest and juice, garlic, cilantro, scallions, cumin, and 1 tablespoon of olive oil in a blender or food processor. Pulse until chunky.

2. Transfer the marinade to a bowl and add the fish. Let the fish marinate for 15 minutes.

3. Heat the remaining 1 tablespoon of olive oil in a nonstick skillet over medium-high heat. Cook the fish, turning once or twice, until it is opaque and flakes easily with a fork, about 5 minutes.

4. Heat the tortillas in the microwave, wrapped in a damp paper towel, or in a lightly greased skillet over medium heat. Divide the fish among the tortillas and top with the salsa.

Complete the Plate: This meal completes the plate, but could still use even more vegetables. I love serving my fish tacos with the Crisp Cucumber and Lime Salad (page 142), the Fiesta Salad (page 144), or the Classic Creamy Picnic Coleslaw (page 146).

Grilled Swordfish Kebabs

SERVES 4 (1 KEBAB EACH) Swordfish is a firm fish that is perfect for cooking in a grill pan or directly on an outdoor grill. In a pinch, you can even use your oven's broiler to achieve similarly delicious results. While eggplant isn't often seen on kebabs, it's fantastic when marinated and grilled, as it picks up the bold marinade flavors and transforms into a creamy, smoky complement to the fish.

FULL PLATE

PREP TIME:
15 minutes +
30 minutes to
marinate

COOK TIME:
8 minutes

PER SERVING:
Calories: 267
Total fat: 8g
Saturated fat: 2g
Cholesterol: 75mg
Sodium: 600mg
Carbs: 25g
Fiber: 10g
Sugars: 13g
Protein: 26g

1 tablespoon freshly grated lemon zest

½ cup freshly squeezed lemon juice

2 garlic cloves, minced

1 tablespoon fish sauce

1 tablespoon honey

¼ teaspoon salt

½ teaspoon red pepper flakes

1 pound swordfish, cut into cubes

3 small Japanese eggplants, cut into 2-inch chunks

8 ounces cherry tomatoes

2 tablespoons finely shredded fresh mint, for garnish

1. In a mixing bowl, whisk together the lemon zest and juice, garlic, fish sauce, honey, salt, and red pepper flakes. Add the fish and eggplants. Cover and refrigerate for 30 minutes.

2. Preheat the grill to medium-high.

3. Remove the fish from the marinade, reserving the marinade. Thread the fish, eggplant, and cherry tomatoes onto the skewers, alternating as you go.

4. Grill the skewers, brushing occasionally with the reserved marinade, until the fish is cooked through, flipping three times so that each of the four sides of the swordfish cubes sits on the grill for about 2 minutes. Garnish with the mint and serve.

Complete the Plate: While this recipe completes the plate, it's a good idea to serve with a Fiesta Salad (page 144) or Black-Eyed Peas and Kale Salad (page 171) to get some more high-quality carbs, and a Simple Green Salad with Garlic, Lemon, and Olive Oil Vinaigrette (page 145) or Sweet and Tender Kale Salad (page 143) to include more leafy greens.

eat what you love DIABETES COOKBOOK

Oven-Baked "Fried" Whitefish

¼ PLATE

PREP TIME:
10 minutes

COOK TIME:
20 minutes

PER SERVING:
Calories: 264
Total fat: 13g
Saturated fat: 3g
Cholesterol: 76mg
Sodium: 59mg
Carbs: 11g
Fiber: 2g
Sugars: 0g
Protein: 24g

SERVES 4 (4 OUNCES EACH) Frying fish loads on unnecessary fat from cooking oil, but in this "oven-fried" recipe, you can achieve the same browned, crisp crust without the added fat and calories. Quinoa bread crumbs create a crisp crust, and a small amount of butter helps brown the exterior. Use any white fish you like, such as haddock, cod, or tilapia.

1 pound firm white fish fillets

1 tablespoon organic canola oil

Grated zest and juice of 1 lemon

½ teaspoon onion powder

½ teaspoon garlic powder

½ teaspoon freshly ground black pepper

¼ cup whole-wheat bread crumbs

¼ cup cooked quinoa or additional ¼ cup whole-wheat bread crumbs

1 tablespoon unsalted butter, melted

1. Preheat the oven to 425ºF. Line a baking sheet with parchment paper.

2. Place the fish on a plate. Drizzle each fillet with oil and lemon juice and sprinkle the lemon zest, onion powder, garlic powder, and pepper on top.

3. Combine the bread crumbs on a plate, and gently roll each fillet in the bread crumbs, pressing them into the surface. Transfer the fish to the lined baking sheet. Drizzle with the melted butter.

4. Bake until the bread crumbs are browned and the fish flakes easily, 15 to 20 minutes.

Tip: You can prep these fillets in advance by following the recipe through step 3. When complete, place the baking sheet in the freezer and leave for at least 1 to 3 hours. Pack the frozen fish pieces in a freezer-safe bag or container. When ready to use, bake until cooked through, browned, and crisp, 25 to 30 minutes.

Complete the Plate: Serve with a vegetable such as Summer Strawberry-Arugula Salad (page 141) or Five-Minute Brussels Sprouts and Almonds (page 154) and a starchy side such as Crispy Sage-Roasted Root Vegetables (page 165) or Macaroni and Cheese with Mixed Vegetables (page 178).

eat what you love DIABETES COOKBOOK

Shrimp Boil

SERVES 4 (2 CORN PIECES + 6 SHRIMP EACH) Dinner can't get much simpler than this. A boil is super easy to throw together and results in a tasty meal in no time. Seasoning is key, and here we combine everyday spices and herbs to make a savory blend with a little kick. Top the shrimp, potatoes, and corn with a squeeze of lemon juice, and you have a ready-to-go meal that shines.

4 bay leaves

2 teaspoons paprika

2 teaspoons garlic powder

1 teaspoon cayenne pepper

½ teaspoon freshly ground black pepper

½ teaspoon mustard powder

2 ears corn, shucked and quartered

1 pound large shrimp, peeled and deveined but tails left on

2 lemons, cut into wedges

½ PLATE

PREP TIME:
10 minutes

COOK TIME:
16 minutes

PER SERVING:
Calories: 133
Total fat: 2g
Saturated fat: 0g
Cholesterol:
143mg
Sodium: 662mg
Carbs: 14g
Fiber: 3g
Sugars: 2g
Protein: 17g

1. Bring a large pot of water to a boil over medium-high heat. Add the bay leaves, paprika, garlic powder, cayenne pepper, black pepper, and mustard powder. Cover and simmer for 10 minutes.

2. Add the corn to the pot and cook, uncovered, for 3 minutes. Add the shrimp and cook until opaque and pink, about 3 minutes more. Use a slotted spoon to transfer the shrimp and corn to individual serving dishes. Serve hot, with lemon wedges to squeeze over everything.

Complete the Plate: In order to complete the plate, more vegetables are needed. Add the Simple Green Salad with Garlic, Lemon, and Olive Oil Vinaigrette (page 145) or Sweet and Tender Kale Salad (page 143). You can also add an additional serving of starch or grains.

Lemon-Garlic Shrimp Skewers over Caesar Salad

FULL PLATE

PREP TIME:
15 minutes +
10 minutes to
marinate

COOK TIME:
10 minutes

PER SERVING:
Calories: 304
Total fat: 14g
Saturated fat: 3g
Cholesterol:
154mg
Sodium: 1013mg
Carbs: 23g
Fiber: 5g
Sugars: 3g
Protein: 24g

SERVES 4 (2 CUPS SALAD + 1 SHRIMP SKEWER EACH) Crisp romaine lettuce tossed with a creamy yogurt-based dressing is a pairing that always soothes. Skip store-bought dressings laden with preservatives and fillers, and try this simple, no-nonsense recipe that expertly coats the lettuce with flavor and umami. Even if you are convinced that you don't like anchovies, try them here—this key Caesar salad ingredient melds into the dressing, leaving little fishy flavor.

FOR THE CROUTONS

4 slices high-fiber whole-grain bread

1 teaspoon extra-virgin olive oil

1 large garlic clove, peeled and halved

FOR THE SHRIMP

1 pound large shrimp, peeled and deveined

3 tablespoons freshly squeezed lemon juice

1 tablespoon extra-virgin olive oil

3 garlic cloves, minced

½ teaspoon freshly ground black pepper

FOR THE SALAD

¼ cup plain 2% Greek yogurt

1 tablespoon extra-virgin olive oil

2 tablespoons freshly squeezed lemon juice

1 teaspoon anchovy paste

½ teaspoon Dijon mustard

2 garlic cloves, peeled

8 cups bite-size pieces romaine lettuce

1 large cucumber, halved lengthwise and thinly sliced crosswise

¼ cup grated Parmesan cheese

TO MAKE THE CROUTONS

1. Preheat the oven to 325°F.

2. Using a pastry brush, brush the bread with the olive oil. Rub the cut sides of the garlic clove over the bread firmly on both sides. Cut the bread into 1-inch cubes.

3. Spread out the cubes on a baking sheet and bake, stirring once or twice, until crisp and browned, about 10 minutes.

eat what you love DIABETES COOKBOOK

TO MAKE THE SHRIMP

1. In a small bowl, toss the shrimp with the lemon juice, olive oil, garlic, and pepper. Mix well and set aside to marinate for 10 minutes.

2. Preheat the broiler to high.

3. Thread the shrimp onto four skewers and place the skewers on a baking sheet.

4. Place the baking sheet under the broiler and broil, flipping once, until the shrimp turn pink, 3 to 5 minutes per side. Remove and set aside.

TO MAKE THE SALAD

1. In a small bowl, whisk together the yogurt, olive oil, lemon juice, anchovy paste, mustard, and garlic.

2. In a large bowl, toss the dressing with the lettuce and cucumber until well coated.

3. Add the croutons and Parmesan cheese and toss again to integrate. Divide the salad among four plates and top each with a shrimp skewer. Serve.

Tip: If using wooden skewers for the shrimp, be sure to soak them in water for 30 minutes before threading. If using metal skewers, oil them lightly before threading.

Complete the Plate: While this recipe completes the plate, you can add a small serving of your favorite starch or grain side. I love to add the Old-Fashioned Sweet Potato Bake with Pecans (page 166) or the Mediterranean Oven-Roasted Potatoes and Vegetables with Herbs (page 168).

Crab Cakes

SERVES 4 (2 CRAB CAKES EACH) Crabmeat is a lean selection that is finger-licking good, especially when pan-fried into these tasty cakes. Be sure not to overmix the ingredients, as the lumps of crabmeat are one of the best aspects of this simple dish.

1 large egg

2 tablespoons plain 2% Greek yogurt

¼ cup whole-wheat bread crumbs

2 tablespoons chopped fresh parsley

1 teaspoon grated lemon zest

½ teaspoon freshly ground black pepper

1 pound lump crabmeat

1 tablespoon extra-virgin olive oil

2 lemons, cut into wedges, for serving

¼ **PLATE**

PREP TIME:
20 minutes

COOK TIME:
15 minutes

PER SERVING:
Calories: 193
Total fat: 7g
Saturated fat: 2g
Cholesterol:
120mg
Sodium: 363mg
Carbs: 9g
Fiber: 2g
Sugars: 1g
Protein: 24g

1. In a mixing bowl, combine the egg, yogurt, bread crumbs, parsley, lemon zest, and pepper. Mix well. Gently fold in the crabmeat, working to incorporate it without breaking up the large pieces.

2. Shape the mixture into 8 balls and flatten them into patties. Arrange these on a plate and refrigerate for 10 minutes.

3. In a large skillet, heat the olive oil over medium heat. Add the crab cakes to the pan and cook until nicely browned and cooked through, 6 to 7 minutes per side. Remove from the pan and serve hot, with the lemon wedges.

Complete the Plate: Serve with a vegetable side such as Sweet and Tender Kale Salad (page 143) or Roasted Beets and Greens with Balsamic Dressing (page 161) and a starch side such as Crispy Sage-Roasted Root Vegetables (page 165) or Mashed Cauliflower and Potatoes (page 170).

Shrimp Zoodle Scampi

SERVES 4 (1½ CUPS ZOODLES + 6 SHRIMP EACH) Shrimp scampi is typically served atop a generous portion of white pasta, which doesn't make it low-carb friendly. Using zoodles in place of traditional pasta, however, keeps the carbohydrate count low and allows you to enjoy this luxurious dish anytime.

¾ PLATE

PREP TIME:
10 minutes

COOK TIME:
10 minutes

PER SERVING:
Calories: 199
Total fat: 10g
Saturated fat: 3g
Cholesterol:
150mg
Sodium: 650mg
Carbs: 9g
Fiber: 3g
Sugars: 0g
Protein: 22g

4 medium zucchini (about 2 pounds)

1 tablespoon unsalted butter

4 teaspoons extra-virgin olive oil, divided

6 garlic cloves, minced

1 pound large shrimp, peeled and deveined

¼ teaspoon freshly ground black pepper

2 tablespoons chopped fresh parsley

¼ cup freshly squeezed lemon juice (from 2 or 3 lemons)

Pinch red pepper flakes

1. Using a spiralizer, cut the zucchini into noodles 4 to 6 inches long. Set aside.

2. In a large skillet, heat the butter and 2 teaspoons of olive oil over medium-high heat. Add the garlic and sauté until fragrant. Add the shrimp and pepper and cook, stirring frequently, until the shrimp turn opaque and pink, about 5 minutes. Transfer the shrimp to a plate.

3. In the same skillet, heat the remaining 2 teaspoons of olive oil over medium-high heat. Add the zoodles to the pan and cook, stirring frequently, for 2 minutes. Remove the skillet from the heat and stir in the shrimp, parsley, lemon juice, and red pepper flakes. Serve.

Tip: Be sure not to cook the zoodles for more than 2 minutes; if they are cooked longer, they will become watery and start to fall apart.

Complete the Plate: Pair with Mashed Cauliflower and Potatoes (page 170) or Sweet Potato Fries (page 167).

eat what you love DIABETES COOKBOOK

Spicy Seafood Stew

SERVES 8 (1½ CUPS EACH) Crab and shrimp combine in this tomato-based stew that is bursting with flavor and spice. Although this meal can be on the table in under an hour, it benefits from a resting period, so it is even better made a day in advance and then chilled to allow the flavors to meld.

1 teaspoon organic canola oil

1 yellow onion, diced

2 green bell peppers, seeded and diced

2 pounds medium shrimp, peeled and deveined

2 (6-ounce) cans lump crabmeat, picked over

2 (28-ounce) cans no-salt-added diced tomatoes, undrained

4 tablespoons unsalted butter, divided

1 teaspoon honey

1 teaspoon garlic powder

1 teaspoon cayenne pepper

¾ PLATE

PREP TIME:
10 minutes

COOK TIME:
45 minutes

PER SERVING:
Calories: 205
Total fat: 8g
Saturated fat: 4g
Cholesterol:
188mg
Sodium: 780mg
Carbs: 10g
Fiber: 3g
Sugars: 5g
Protein: 22g

1. In a large Dutch oven, heat the canola oil over medium heat. Add the onion and green peppers and sauté until soft, 3 to 4 minutes. Add the shrimp, crabmeat, tomatoes (with their juice), and 2 tablespoons of butter. Bring to a simmer and cook, stirring occasionally, for 30 minutes.

2. Add the remaining 2 tablespoons of butter, the honey, the garlic powder, and the cayenne. Taste and adjust the seasonings as needed.

Tip: This is a versatile stew that can be adjusted with different proteins according to personal preference. Chicken wings, crawfish tails, and firm white fish can all be substituted in similar proportions for the shrimp or crabmeat, if desired.

Complete the Plate: Serve over ½ cup of quinoa or ⅔ cup of brown rice. And I've never known someone to eat too many vegetables, so feel free to include a green salad or your favorite roasted nonstarchy vegetables also.

Pasta with
Sun-Dried
Tomatoes,
Feta Cheese,
and Arugula

Meatless Mains

The hearty meals you will find in this chapter are packed with all the "good stuff"—vegetables, beans, whole grains, and healthy fats are highlighted throughout. All the meatless mains here are low in cholesterol and high in fiber, so they are a great choice to eat any day of the week. Because fiber helps slow the digestion of food, these dishes are less likely to spike blood sugar and will keep us full for longer periods of time. The result? Delicious meals that lower blood sugar, cholesterol, and even our waistlines. A perfect combination!

The recipes in this section don't require lots of time in the kitchen, in the hopes you'll make these meatless mains often. So look forward to warming soups, noodles, zoodles, and more!

Warming Vegetable Lentil Soup

SERVES 6 (2 CUPS EACH) Everyone can use a hearty soup recipe they can serve year-round. This is the go-to soup I prepare for my friends and family if they are in need of a nourishing meal. Whether it's a new baby, a seasonal cold, or just a busy week, this soup hits the spot. It provides protein, fiber, vegetables, and hydration, all packed in a simple dish.

FULL PLATE

PREP TIME:
15 minutes

COOK TIME:
1 hour

PER SERVING:
Calories: 295
Total fat: 6g
Saturated fat: 1g
Cholesterol: 0mg
Sodium: 367mg
Carbs: 47g
Fiber: 20g
Sugars: 8g
Protein: 16g

2 tablespoons extra-virgin olive oil

1 onion, chopped

3 celery stalks, chopped

3 carrots, peeled and diced

1 cup cut-up green beans (1-inch pieces)

3 or 4 garlic cloves, minced

1 teaspoon ground turmeric

1 teaspoon dried thyme

½ teaspoon salt

½ teaspoon freshly ground black pepper

¼ teaspoon red pepper flakes (optional)

4 cups water

4 cups low-sodium vegetable broth

1½ cup lentils

1 cup fresh or frozen green peas

1 pound Roma tomatoes (about 5 tomatoes), diced

2 cups chopped kale

¼ cup grated Parmesan cheese (optional)

1. Heat the olive oil in a large pot over medium heat. Add the onion, celery, carrots, and green beans. Cook until the vegetables have softened, 4 to 6 minutes.

2. Add the garlic, turmeric, thyme, salt, black pepper, and red pepper flakes (if using), and cook for another 1 minute.

3. Add the water, broth, lentils, peas, and tomatoes. Raise the heat to high to bring to a boil. Then reduce the heat to low and simmer for 45 minutes.

4. Stir in the kale and simmer for an additional 10 minutes.

5. Spoon into bowls and top with Parmesan cheese (if using) and additional black pepper, if desired.

Tip: Green peas are high in a trace mineral called chromium, which works with insulin to help use blood sugar for energy. This recipe provides 10 micrograms of chromium per serving, of the recommended 25 to 35 micrograms per day.

Kabocha and Carrot Soup

SERVES 6 (1 CUP EACH) Kabocha is a Japanese squash with showy orange flesh and a soft, creamy texture, making it a perfect backdrop for a wonderful bowl of creamy soup. Blended with carrots for even more complexity, this soup is both filling and nutritious. Double the recipe and store some in the freezer in individual serving sizes for a quick meal when you are too busy to cook it from scratch.

¾ PLATE

PREP TIME:
15 minutes

COOK TIME:
1 hour 20 minutes

PER SERVING:
Calories: 160
Total fat: 5g
Saturated fat: 1g
Cholesterol: 0mg
Sodium: 336mg
Carbs: 29g
Fiber: 6g
Sugars: 8g
Protein: 3g

½ large (3-pound) kabocha squash

2 tablespoons extra-virgin olive oil, divided

2 cups sliced carrots

1 cup chopped onions

2 celery stalks, chopped

2-inch knob ginger, peeled and grated

1½ teaspoons ground cumin

½ teaspoon ground coriander

2 (14.5-ounce) cans low-sodium vegetable broth

½ teaspoon salt

½ teaspoon freshly ground black pepper

¼ cup unsweetened almond milk

1. Preheat the oven to 400°F.

2. Scoop the seeds out of the kabocha half. Using a sharp knife, cut the kabocha into 3 or 4 large pieces. Rub with 1 tablespoon of olive oil and place on a baking sheet. Roast until the flesh is tender and the edges are beginning to brown, 45 to 60 minutes.

3. In a large pot, heat the remaining 1 tablespoon of olive oil over medium-high heat. Add the carrots, onions, and celery and cook, stirring frequently, until softened, about 10 minutes. Add the ginger, cumin, and coriander and cook for 2 more minutes.

4. Add the vegetable broth, salt, and pepper. Bring to a boil and then reduce the heat to a simmer.

5. Once the kabocha is cool enough to handle, slip the flesh from its skin and add it to the soup. Use an immersion blender to purée the soup right in the pot, or work in batches puréeing it in a blender.

6. Add the almond milk and stir until heated through. Serve.

Complete the Plate: Serve with Cinnamon-Citrus Cod (page 109) or Cashew and Parmesan Crusted Salmon (page 107).

eat what you love DIABETES COOKBOOK

Barley and Bean Soup

SERVES 4 (1½ CUPS EACH) This soup draws on the classic, comforting flavors of a good minestrone soup, but without any starchy pasta in sight. Instead, it features barley, a whole grain that thickens and adds a wonderful texture to this simple soup. Leave it to simmer, and your kitchen will smell fantastic.

⅓ cup hulled barley

2 cups water

1 tablespoon extra-virgin olive oil

1 large onion, diced

4 garlic cloves, minced

4 cups low-sodium vegetable broth

1 cup diced tomatoes

1 (15-ounce) can cannellini beans, rinsed and drained

3 cups torn kale

½ teaspoon salt

¼ teaspoon freshly ground black pepper

¼ cup fresh cilantro leaves, for garnish

¼ cup fresh mint leaves, for garnish

FULL PLATE

PREP TIME:
10 minutes

COOK TIME:
45 minutes

PER SERVING:
Calories: 264
Total fat: 5g
Saturated fat: 1g
Cholesterol: 0mg
Sodium: 504mg
Carbs: 46g
Fiber: 12g
Sugars: 5g
Protein: 11g

1. In a small saucepan, combine the barley and water and bring to a boil over medium-high heat. Reduce the heat, cover, and simmer for 20 minutes. Drain and set aside.

2. In a large Dutch oven, heat the oil over medium-high heat. Add the onion and cook, stirring constantly, until it begins to soften, about 3 minutes. Add the garlic and cook for 1 minute.

3. Add the broth, tomatoes, and beans. Bring to a simmer and cook for 10 minutes.

4. Add the kale and barley and cook until tender, about 10 more minutes. Add the salt and pepper.

5. Serve, garnished with the cilantro and mint leaves.

Complete the Plate: While this recipe contains all the elements of a complete meal, you may want to add more protein and nonstarchy vegetables to ensure you are full and energized. I enjoy combining this soup with the Miso Salmon (page 108) and Cauliflower Rice (page 149).

Hearty Vegan Slow Cooker Chili

FULL PLATE

PREP TIME:
10 minutes

COOK TIME:
3 to 4 hours or
6 to 8 hours

PER SERVING:
Calories: 205
Total fat: 1g
Saturated fat: <1g
Cholesterol: 0mg
Sodium: 275mg
Carbs: 40g
Fiber: 13g
Sugars: 10g
Protein: 10g

SERVES 4 (1½ CUPS EACH) When the weather starts cooling down in the fall, it's time to prepare some hearty and comforting chili in the slow cooker—my favorite time-saver in the kitchen. This recipe is easy to throw together, yet represents a powerhouse of superfoods. Don't be surprised if you find yourself wanting leftovers for breakfast, lunch, and dinner!

1 (15-ounce) can no-salt added red kidney beans, rinsed and drained

1 (14.5-ounce) can no-salt-added diced tomatoes, undrained

1 medium sweet potato, peeled and diced

1 cup water

3 celery stalks, diced

1 red or yellow bell pepper, seeded and diced

1 small onion, diced

2 or 3 garlic cloves, minced

2 tablespoons chili powder

1 tablespoon dried oregano

2 teaspoons ground cumin

Pinch cayenne pepper

2 teaspoons chopped fresh cilantro, for garnish

Dollop plain 2% Greek yogurt (optional), for garnish

In a slow cooker, combine all the ingredients except the garnishes. Cover and cook on low for 6 to 8 hours or on high for 3 to 4 hours. Serve garnished with cilantro and Greek yogurt (if using).

Tip: Each serving of this recipe contains ½ cup of beans, which supplies one-third of your daily requirement of fiber. The beans are also high in potassium, which is helpful in maintaining regular blood pressure.

Complete the Plate: While this recipe meets the balanced-plate requirements, you can add an additional serving of protein or nonstarchy vegetables to make sure you are satisfied until your next meal.

Mushroom Burgers

SERVES 2 (1 BURGER EACH) This was one of the first savory recipes I made when I began cooking for myself and exploring healthier options in the kitchen. It's very affordable and easily adapted to make a single serving, if needed. If you are short on time, you can skip marinating the mushrooms and just go ahead and start cooking.

FULL PLATE

PREP TIME:
10 minutes +
30 minutes to
marinate

COOK TIME:
6 to 8 minutes

PER SERVING:
Calories: 365
Total fat: 17g
Saturated fat: 6g
Cholesterol: 19mg
Sodium: 697mg
Carbs: 37g
Fiber: 7g
Sugars: 8g
Protein: 17g

2 tablespoons balsamic vinegar

1 tablespoon extra-virgin olive oil

2 teaspoons Dijon mustard, plus 1 teaspoon for the buns (optional)

Freshly ground black pepper

2 portobello mushrooms, stemmed

1 red bell pepper, seeded and cut into ¼-inch-thick rings

2 whole-wheat buns

2 provolone cheese slices (optional)

½ cup baby spinach

2 red onion slices

2 tomato slices

1. In a zip-top bag, combine the vinegar, olive oil, mustard, and a pinch of black pepper. Add the mushrooms and bell pepper. Let marinate at room temperature for 30 minutes.

2. Heat a skillet over medium-high heat. Add the mushrooms, bell pepper, and remaining marinade to the skillet. Cook the vegetables for 3 to 4 minutes on each side.

3. Divide the vegetables between the buns. Add the provolone cheese (if using). Top with the spinach, onion, and tomato. Add additional Dijon mustard (if using) to the buns.

Complete the Plate: While this meal completes the balanced plate, it would be great to serve it with an additional vegetable side. I enjoy adding the Roasted Beets and Greens with Balsamic Dressing (page 161).

Crisp Vegetable and Quinoa Bowl

SERVES 4 (3 CUPS EACH) Quinoa pairs well with just about any vegetable you want to throw at it. Here, a medley of green vegetables—asparagus, peas, cucumber, and spinach—fill out the bowl with plenty of crunch. Topped with a creamy garlicky dressing, this comforting meal will fill you up without feeling too heavy.

FULL PLATE

PREP TIME:
15 minutes

COOK TIME:
12 minutes

PER SERVING:
Calories: 462
Total fat: 25g
Saturated fat: 4g
Cholesterol: 4mg
Sodium: 420mg
Carbs: 47g
Fiber: 10g
Sugars: 6g
Protein: 19g

¾ cup plain 2% Greek yogurt

¼ cup freshly squeezed lemon juice

2 tablespoons extra-virgin olive oil

6 garlic cloves, minced

½ teaspoon salt

1 cup quinoa

2 cups water

1 pound asparagus, cut into 2-inch pieces

1 cup fresh or frozen green peas

1 cucumber, peeled, halved lengthwise, and thinly sliced crosswise

8 cups baby spinach

½ cup walnut pieces

1. In a small bowl, whisk together the yogurt, lemon juice, olive oil, garlic, and salt. Set aside.

2. In a small pot, combine the quinoa and water. Bring to a boil over medium-high heat, reduce the heat, cover, and simmer until tender, about 10 minutes. Drain any remaining water and spread out the quinoa on a baking sheet to cool.

3. Bring a large pot of water to a boil over medium-high heat. Add the asparagus and peas and cook until they are crisp-tender, about 2 minutes. Drain and run the vegetables under cold water to stop them from cooking.

4. Divide the quinoa among four bowls. Top each bowl with equal amounts of asparagus, peas, cucumber, spinach, and walnuts. Drizzle the dressing over the bowls and serve.

Tip: For easy prep of salads like this, cook double the amount of quinoa needed and store the extra in an airtight container in the refrigerator for up to 5 days. When needed, simply cut the veggies, make the dressing, and toss with the quinoa for a healthy version of fast food.

Broccoli-Almond-Sesame Soba Noodles

SERVES 4 (1½ CUPS EACH) A bowl of tasty noodles is a classic comfort for many, though for those with diabetes, the starchy nature of wheat noodles makes them prohibitive. This reworked version uses buckwheat soba noodles paired with a flavorful sesame dressing that makes them just as comforting as your favorite Alfredo—just without all the added fat and carbohydrates. Be sure to rinse the noodles under cold water after cooking, as this prevents clumping.

FULL PLATE

PREP TIME:
10 minutes +
1 hour to chill

COOK TIME:
15 minutes

PER SERVING:
Calories: 247
Total fat: 6g
Saturated fat: 1g
Cholesterol: 0mg
Sodium: 749mg
Carbs: 10g
Fiber: 3g
Sugars: 6g
Protein: 7g

¼ cup sliced almonds

6-ounces dried buckwheat soba noodles

1 cup fresh or frozen broccoli florets

2 tablespoons low-sodium soy sauce

1 tablespoon rice vinegar

2 teaspoons honey

2 teaspoons toasted sesame oil

½ cup sliced sugar snap or snow peas

1 bunch scallions (green and white parts), finely chopped

1 red bell pepper, seeded and sliced

1. Heat a small skillet over medium-high heat. Toast the almonds, shaking the pan continuously, until just browned, 2 to 3 minutes. Remove from the pan and set aside.

2. Bring a large pot of water to a boil over high heat. Add the noodles. Cook according to the package directions. Drain the noodles and immediately run them under cold water until cool to the touch. Transfer to a large bowl.

3. Meanwhile, fill another large pot with a couple of inches of water and a steaming basket. Bring the water to a boil over high heat and add the broccoli. Cover and steam the broccoli until fork-tender yet still bright green, 3 to 5 minutes. Remove the broccoli from the basket and run it under cold water until cool. Transfer to the bowl with the noodles. ▶

4. In a small bowl, whisk together the soy sauce, rice vinegar, honey, and sesame oil.

5. Add the peas, scallions, bell pepper, almonds, and soy sauce mixture to the noodles and broccoli. Toss well to combine. Refrigerate for at least 1 hour before serving to allow the flavors to meld.

Tip: Be sure to read the label when buying buckwheat soba. Unless the label specifically states "100% buckwheat soba," it likely contains other grains, namely wheat. Look for brands that contain only buckwheat at health food stores, Asian grocers, and online.

Complete the Plate: While this dish contains all the plate elements, you may want to add an additional source of protein. Keep it simple with a grilled or baked serving of your favorite lean protein.

Creamy Pesto Zoodles

SERVES 4 (2 CUPS EACH) Pesto sauce is creamy, delightful, and surprisingly easy to make. This version uses walnuts in place of the more traditional pine nuts, for both their lower cost and higher content of omega-3 fatty acids. Simple and quick to prepare, this raw meal can be on the table in less than 15 minutes.

4 small zucchini

2 cups packed fresh basil leaves

2 garlic cloves, peeled

¼ cup walnuts

¼ cup extra-virgin olive oil

½ teaspoon salt

¼ teaspoon freshly ground black pepper

¼ cup grated Parmesan cheese

1 cup cherry tomatoes, halved

½ **PLATE**

PREP TIME:
15 minutes

PER SERVING:
Calories: 240
Total fat: 21g
Saturated fat: 4g
Cholesterol: 6mg
Sodium: 405mg
Carbs: 10g
Fiber: 3g
Sugars: 6g
Protein: 7g

1. Using a spiralizer, cut the zucchini into noodles 4 to 6 inches long.

2. In a food processor, combine the basil, garlic, walnuts, olive oil, salt, and pepper. Process until smooth. Add the Parmesan cheese and pulse once or twice to mix.

3. Transfer the pesto to a large bowl and add the zoodles. Toss to combine. Add the tomatoes and toss again. Serve.

Tip: If you prefer, the zoodles can be cooked before mixing. To do this, heat 1 teaspoon extra-virgin olive oil in a large skillet and sauté the zucchini until just tender, about 2 minutes. Remove from the heat and toss with the pesto.

Complete the Plate: Serve with 3 to 4 ounces of your favorite lean protein. Also add a serving of your favorite fruit or a starch/grain side such as Mashed Cauliflower and Potatoes (page 170).

Cheesy Garlic Pasta Salad

SERVES 4 (1¼ CUPS EACH) So many people tell me they didn't realize they could still eat pasta after a diabetes diagnosis—this recipe shows you how! This tempting recipe offers the perfect combination of nourishing vegetables and comforting pasta. This dish doesn't sacrifice any flavor and even gets better after a day or two in the refrigerator—if it lasts that long!

FULL PLATE

PREP TIME:
5 to 10 minutes

COOK TIME:
5 minutes

PER SERVING:
Calories: 212
Total fat: 7g
Saturated fat: 4g
Cholesterol: 10mg
Sodium: 158mg
Carbs: 30g
Fiber: 4g
Sugars: 3g
Protein: 11g

6 asparagus spears, trimmed and cut into 1-inch pieces

1 teaspoon extra-virgin olive oil

Freshly ground black pepper

3 cups cooked whole-wheat penne pasta

3 ounces goat cheese

¾ cup cherry tomatoes, quartered

½ cup diced yellow bell pepper

2 garlic cloves, minced

1 cup chopped arugula

3 large basil leaves, minced

Pinch salt

1. Preheat the broiler on high. Line a baking sheet with aluminum foil.

2. Put the asparagus on the lined baking sheet. Drizzle with the olive oil and season with black pepper. Broil for 5 minutes.

3. If the pasta is not already warm, heat in the microwave for about 30 seconds. Put the pasta in a large mixing bowl. Add the goat cheese, tomatoes, bell pepper, garlic, arugula, and basil. Stir to combine well.

4. Add the asparagus to the pasta mixture. Season with a pinch each of salt and freshly ground pepper.

Complete the Plate: While this dish satisfies all of the requirements of a full plate, I would still recommend adding an additional serving of lean protein and non-starchy vegetables.

Pasta with Sun-Dried Tomatoes, Feta Cheese, and Arugula

FULL PLATE

PREP TIME:
5 minutes

COOK TIME:
10 minutes

PER SERVING:
Calories: 217
Total fat: 7g
Saturated fat: 1g
Cholesterol: 0mg
Sodium: 352mg
Carbs: 31g
Fiber: 5g
Sugars: 3g
Protein: 9g

SERVES 4 (1 CUP EACH) This quick and comforting meal is perfect for a busy weeknight when you need dinner on the table in under 20 minutes. Featuring simple ingredients, this dish is a standout for both its ease of preparation and enticing, earthy flavors. Arugula contributes a spicy undertone, while sun-dried tomatoes and feta provide the comfort-food flavors you love.

½ pound whole-wheat penne pasta

2 tablespoons extra-virgin olive oil

3 garlic cloves, minced

½ cup sun-dried tomatoes

½ cup reduced-fat feta cheese, crumbled

¼ teaspoon salt

¼ teaspoon freshly ground black pepper

3 cups arugula

1. Bring a large pot of water to a boil over high heat. Cook the pasta according to the package directions. Drain.

2. In a large skillet, heat the olive oil over medium-high heat. Add the garlic and sauté until just fragrant. Add the sun-dried tomatoes and cook for 1 additional minute, stirring constantly.

3. Add the cooked noodles to the skillet and sprinkle with the feta cheese, salt, and pepper. Stir to combine. Add the arugula, toss, and serve.

Complete the Plate: This is a recipe that would be great with an additional serving of vegetables. Serve with Sautéed Garlic, Ginger, and Shallot Green Beans (page 156), Sweet and Tender Kale Salad (page 143), or your favorite nonstarchy roasted vegetables.

Top: Grilled
Zucchini Salad;
Bottom: Crispy
Sage-Roasted Root
Vegetables (chapter 8)

Vegetable Sides

The versatility of vegetables is unlike that of any other type of food, and the health benefits they offer are endless. But they are also comforting and nourishing in their own way. Whether served warm, cold, creamy, roasted, mashed, or puréed, you will notice each manner of preparation offers its own satisfying taste.

Vegetables should be the focus of all your meals. I always tell my clients, "I have yet to meet anyone who eats too many vegetables." Simply put, they are the number one food group, and we should all be eating more! Since vegetables are naturally low in calories and high in fiber, they are the perfect way to create filling, satisfying meals. So complete your plate by ensuring that half of every meal comes from the low-carb vegetables you will find in this chapter. Once you try the veggie recipes here, you probably won't need much convincing any-way—you just might find yourself craving them!

Summer Strawberry-Arugula Salad

SERVES 4 (1¾ CUPS EACH) This salad represents everything I love about summer! Refreshing, light, seasonal ingredients come together in a simple yet delicious salad. Since grilling outside is a great way to amp up any meal, I often grill some lightly marinated fish or chicken to turn this into an entrée salad.

PREP TIME:
5 minutes

COOK TIME:
20 minutes

PER SERVING:
Calories: 129
Total fat: 9g
Saturated fat: 1g
Cholesterol: 0mg
Sodium: 20mg
Carbs: 10g
Fiber: 4g
Sugars: 4g
Protein: 3g

½ cup raw almonds

2 teaspoons extra-virgin olive oil, divided

1 tablespoon dried rosemary

Pinch cayenne pepper

4 cups arugula

4 large fresh basil leaves, chopped

1 cup sliced fresh strawberries, plus 1 mashed strawberry

½ cup sliced cucumbers

¼ cup avocado cubes

½ cup chopped carrots

3 teaspoons balsamic vinegar

1 teaspoon poppy seeds

1. Preheat the oven to 325°F. Line a baking sheet with parchment paper.

2. On the baking sheet, toss the almonds with 1 teaspoon of olive oil, the rosemary, and the cayenne pepper. Bake for 20 minutes, tossing once to make sure the almonds are evenly coated.

3. In a large bowl, combine the arugula, basil, sliced strawberries, cucumbers, avocado, and carrots.

4. In a small bowl, whisk together the balsamic vinegar, remaining 1 teaspoon of olive oil, poppy seeds, and mashed strawberry. Add to the arugula blend and mix well.

5. Once the almonds are finished, let cool for 10 minutes before adding to the top of the salad.

Tip: Berries like the strawberries found in this recipe are the best types of fruits for those with diabetes, as they are low on the glycemic index yet high in satisfying fiber.

Crisp Cucumber and Lime Salad

½ PLATE

PREP TIME:
5 minutes +
15 minutes to chill

PER SERVING:
Calories: 28
Total fat: 0g
Saturated fat: 0g
Cholesterol: 0mg
Sodium: 2mg
Carbs: 7g
Fiber: 2g
Sugars: 3g
Protein: 1g

SERVES 4 (1¼ CUPS EACH) This crowd pleaser is my favorite recipe when I'm looking for a light, refreshing side dish. The blueberries and mint leaves create a colorful combo, while the jicama gives it just the right amount of "crunch." And it's perfect to share or bring with you to the beach, the lake, or a pool party.

½ cup fresh blueberries

1 cup diced cucumber

1 cup diced jicama

4 fresh mint leaves, chopped

Juice of 1 lime

Toss together the blueberries, cucumber, jicama, and mint leaves in a medium mixing bowl. Sprinkle the lime juice over the mixture and toss to blend. Refrigerate for at least 15 minutes prior to serving.

Sweet and Tender Kale Salad

SERVES 4 (1½ CUPS EACH) Let's be honest: I didn't grow up eating kale. I'm guessing most of us didn't. However, it has become a staple in my diet as I have learned how nourishing and versatile it can be. Here it is paired with two comfort-food essentials: cheese and roasted nuts. It's a surprising yet delicious combo that will make you appreciate the sweet and savory taste of natural foods.

1 bunch curly kale

Juice of ½ lemon

1 tablespoon extra-virgin olive oil

½ cup chopped pecans

½ cup pomegranate arils

4 ounces goat cheese, crumbled

Pinch salt

Pinch freshly ground black pepper

1. Wash the kale, remove the stems, and tear the leaves into small pieces. Dry the kale thoroughly and put it in a large bowl.

2. Add the lemon juice and olive oil. Massage the oil and juice into the kale until all the leaves are well coated.

3. Place a small skillet over medium-low heat. Toast the pecans, tossing them often, for 3 to 4 minutes.

4. Add the pecans, pomegranate arils, and goat cheese to the kale. Season with a pinch each of salt and pepper. Lightly toss to combine all the ingredients.

Tip: Kale is an important source of vitamin K, which helps clot our blood when we get a cut. Combining it with the healthy fat from olive oil increases the absorption to provide the maximum benefit to our bodies.

½ PLATE

PREP TIME:
10 minutes

COOK TIME:
5 minutes

PER SERVING:
Calories: 241
Total fat: 20g
Saturated fat: 6g
Cholesterol: 13mg
Sodium: 196mg
Carbs: 11g
Fiber: 4g
Sugars: 5g
Protein: 8g

Fiesta Salad

SERVES 4 (1½ CUPS EACH) My personal philosophy is that healthy foods should never be too complicated or time-consuming, because that would make them difficult to incorporate into your daily routine. This salad provides fiber, protein, slow-digesting carbs, and plenty of nutrients. I love to serve it as an appetizer, dip, or simple addition to any meal.

½ **PLATE**

PREP TIME:
5 minutes

PER SERVING:
Calories: 112
Total fat: 4g
Saturated fat: 0g
Cholesterol: 0mg
Sodium: 5mg
Carbs: 16g
Fiber: 6g
Sugars: 2g
Protein: 5g

1 cup cooked or canned black beans, rinsed and drained

1 heirloom tomato, chopped

1 green bell pepper, seeded and diced

½ avocado, diced

1 tablespoon minced jalapeño

Pinch freshly ground black pepper

Pinch cayenne pepper

2 tablespoons chopped fresh cilantro

Juice of 1 lime

Simply toss together all the ingredients in a bowl and enjoy!

Tip: Tomatoes are a superfood for individuals with diabetes. Many people don't realize that tomatoes are a fantastic source of vitamin C, helping our body absorb iron and heal cuts. It also acts as an antioxidant to prevent damage to our bodies' cells.

Simple Green Salad with Garlic, Lemon, and Olive Oil Vinaigrette

½ PLATE

PREP TIME:
10 minutes

PER SERVING:
Calories: 52
Total fat: 4g
Saturated fat: 1g
Cholesterol: 0mg
Sodium: 110mg
Carbs: 5g
Fiber: 2g
Sugars: 1g
Protein: 2g

SERVES 4 (1¾ CUPS EACH) A big green salad is a great way to fill out your plate, especially when you're serving a main course that is plentiful in carbs. This salad is simple to make from scratch and provides a go-to vinaigrette that can be whipped up in minutes any day of the week. Customize the vegetables in the salad to your preferences or whatever you have available, and this salad can be fresh and new each time you prepare it.

1 cup diced or sliced crunchy vegetables (cucumber, bell pepper, radishes, fennel)

1 tablespoon extra-virgin olive oil

3 large garlic cloves, minced

6 cups torn mixed salad greens (romaine, spinach, arugula, red-leaf)

Juice of 1 lemon

⅛ teaspoon salt

⅛ teaspoon freshly ground black pepper

1. In a large bowl, combine the crunchy vegetables, olive oil, and garlic. Toss to combine.

2. Wash the greens well. Use a salad spinner or clean kitchen towel to thoroughly dry the greens. Add the greens to the bowl and toss to combine.

3. Drizzle the lemon juice over the salad and toss to combine. Season lightly with salt and pepper. Serve.

Classic Creamy Picnic Coleslaw

½ PLATE

PREP TIME:
10 minutes

PER SERVING:
Calories: 52
Total fat: 2g
Saturated fat: 1g
Cholesterol: 1mg
Sodium: 326mg
Carbs: 7g
Fiber: 3g
Sugars: 4g
Protein: 2g

SERVES 4 (1 CUP EACH) Coleslaw is a picnic favorite but is typically loaded with extra fat from mayonnaise and buttermilk. This recipe plays on the same creamy texture but achieves it using yogurt instead, adding healthy probiotics to your gut. To mix things up, use a combination of red and green cabbages for a vibrant presentation on the table.

4 cups shredded green cabbage

½ cup shredded carrot

1 teaspoon caraway seeds

½ teaspoon salt

¼ cup plain 2% Greek yogurt

1½ teaspoons freshly squeezed lemon juice

1 teaspoon stone-ground mustard

½ teaspoon honey

1. In a large bowl, toss together the cabbage, carrot, caraway seeds, and salt.

2. In a small bowl, whisk together the yogurt, lemon juice, mustard, and honey. Add the yogurt mixture to the vegetables and mix well to coat. Serve immediately or cover and refrigerate for up to 1 day if made in advance.

Tip: If you are shredding a large amount of cabbage, a mandoline or food processor is very helpful to cut it thinly. If you're cutting it by hand, first remove the core from the cabbage, then cut the head into four equal sections—this will make the cabbage easier to handle.

Fermented Dill Pickles

MAKES 1 QUART (1 PICKLE EACH) If you have never tried fermenting, now is the time to start. These dill pickles are absolutely delicious, and pair wonderfully with any sandwich. Naturally low in carbs, pickles make a great snack, and when you ferment them yourself, you can customize the flavor. Feel free to adapt this recipe as you wish, using different dried or fresh whole herbs or spices—just be sure to keep the same quantity of salt, as this is what protects the cucumbers from spoilage during fermentation.

½ PLATE

PREP TIME:
10 minutes

FERMENTATION TIME:
7 to 10 days

PER SERVING:
Calories: 7
Total fat: <1g
Saturated fat: 0g
Cholesterol: 0mg
Sodium: 785mg
Carbs: 2g
Fiber: <1g
Sugars: <1g
Protein: <1g

1¼ pounds pickling cucumbers

1 dill head

3 garlic cloves, peeled and crushed

1 dried chile pepper, slit lengthwise

5 black peppercorns

1¾ tablespoons pickling salt

2½ cups water

1. Gently wash the cucumbers and remove the blossom end (the end opposite the stem) using a small knife. Put the dill head, garlic, chile, and peppercorns in a quart-size glass jar. Pack the cucumbers snugly into the jar.

2. In a small bowl, mix the salt and water, stirring until the salt is dissolved. Pour the brine over the cucumbers, pressing down on the cucumbers so that they are below the brine. If necessary, use a weight to hold the cucumbers below the brine—a clean shot glass, votive candle holder, or another small jar inserted in the mouth of the jar can all serve as good weights. Cover the jar with a clean kitchen towel secured with a rubber band.

3. Place the jar in a room-temperature location. After a couple of days, bubbles will begin to rise in the jar. Keep an eye on the pickles daily, and skim off any scum that forms on the surface. After 7 to 10 days, the bubbles will stop rising, and then you know the pickles are ready. Place a nonreactive lid on the jar and refrigerate to stop fermentation. The pickles will keep in the fridge for up to 1 month.

Tip: A dill head is the flowering part from the top of the dill plant. You can find it in many grocery stores, or substitute it with 1½ teaspoons dill seeds. Alternatively, try using other seeds such as cumin, fennel, and mustard to create unique pickles your own way.

Cauliflower Rice

SERVES 4 (1 CUP EACH) Like other brassica family vegetables such as broccoli and Brussels sprouts, cauliflower has anticancer, antioxidant, and antiviral properties. Beyond its health benefits, cauliflower takes on the flavor of whatever you throw its way, making it very versatile in the kitchen. This simple faux "rice" is just one of its many uses, and a great way to replace an otherwise starchy side with a more nutritious vegetable. Use this rice substitute anywhere you would normally serve white or brown rice.

½ **PLATE**

PREP TIME:
10 minutes

COOK TIME:
6 minutes

PER SERVING:
Calories: 67
Total fat: 4g
Saturated fat: 1g
Cholesterol: 0mg
Sodium: 44mg
Carbs: 7g
Fiber: 3g
Sugars: 3g
Protein: 3g

1 medium head cauliflower, cut into smaller sections

1 tablespoon olive oil

1. Working in batches, pulse the cauliflower in a food processor until it is in small, rice-size pieces. Transfer the cauliflower to a clean kitchen towel and press firmly to remove any excess water.

2. In a large skillet, heat the olive oil over medium-high heat. Add the cauliflower and sauté for about 1 minute, stirring constantly. Cover, reduce the heat to medium-low, and steam the cauliflower until tender, about 5 minutes.

Tip: If you don't have a food processor, use the largest holes on a box grater to grate the cauliflower into pieces roughly the size of grains of rice.

Vegetable Fried Cauliflower Rice

½ PLATE

PREP TIME:
10 minutes

COOK TIME:
12 minutes

PER SERVING:
Calories: 128
Total fat: 6g
Saturated fat: 1g
Cholesterol:
104mg
Sodium: 383mg
Carbs: 14g
Fiber: 5g
Sugars: 5g
Protein: 8g

SERVES 4 (1½ CUPS EACH) Fried rice is a classic comfort food—an indulgence in salty, starchy, eggy goodness all at once. With this remake using cauliflower rice, you lower the carbs while maintaining all the flavor. Throw this simple side together in about 20 minutes from start to finish, and your body—and taste buds—will thank you for this lighter approach.

1 medium head cauliflower, cut into several sections

2 teaspoons organic canola oil, divided

2 large eggs, beaten

3 garlic cloves, minced

2 medium carrots, peeled and finely diced

¼ cup fresh or frozen peas

4 scallions, thinly sliced

2 tablespoons low-sodium soy sauce

1. Working in batches, pulse the cauliflower in a food processor until it is in small, rice-size pieces. Transfer the cauliflower to a clean kitchen towel and press firmly to remove any excess water.

2. In a large skillet, heat 1 teaspoon of oil over medium-high heat. Pour the beaten eggs into the skillet and use a spatula to scramble them as they cook. Once they are set, transfer the eggs to a small bowl.

3. Add the remaining 1 teaspoon of canola oil to the pan and heat. Add the garlic and cook, stirring constantly, for 30 seconds. Add the carrots and continue cooking and stirring for 2 minutes. Add the peas and cauliflower, stirring to combine. Cover and reduce the heat to medium. Steam until the cauliflower is tender, 5 to 8 minutes.

4. Uncover the skillet and add the scallions and soy sauce. Return the eggs to the pan and stir to combine. Serve hot.

Mexi-Cauli Rice

SERVES 4 (½ CUP EACH) This is one of my favorite dishes to bring to parties, potlucks, and family gatherings. Since it's packed with so much flavor, everyone is always pleasantly surprised to hear it's made with cauliflower. Cauliflower is higher in fiber than white rice, so the dish makes a filling addition to your favorite Mexican meal, a great side dish to serve with any lean protein, or even a healthy snack that won't raise your blood sugar.

3 cups cauliflower florets

1 tablespoon extra-virgin olive oil

½ cup diced onions

⅔ cup sliced tomatoes

1 teaspoon garlic powder

Pinch cayenne pepper

¼ cup chopped fresh cilantro

Juice of ½ lime

⅛ teaspoon salt

⅛ teaspoon freshly ground black pepper

1. In a food processor, pulse the cauliflower a few times until it is in small, rice-like pieces.

2. In a large skillet, heat the olive oil over medium-high heat. Add the cauliflower and onions and sauté until the onions are translucent, 3 to 4 minutes.

3. Add the tomatoes and cook until the tomatoes are broken down, 1 to 2 minutes. Stir in the garlic powder and cayenne pepper and remove from the heat.

4. Stir in the cilantro, lime juice, and salt and pepper. Serve warm.

½ **PLATE**

PREP TIME:
5 minutes

COOK TIME:
5 minutes

PER SERVING:
Calories: 68
Total fat: 4g
Saturated fat: 1g
Cholesterol: 0mg
Sodium: 100mg
Carbs: 8g
Fiber: 2g
Sugars: 3g
Protein: 2g

Broccolini, Yellow Squash, and Radishes with Mustard-Yogurt Dressing

SERVES 4 (1 CUP EACH) Broccolini is a cross between broccoli and Chinese broccoli, taking the best from both worlds to create a tender, sweet hybrid. A quick steam is all this vegetable needs to bring it to the table, and when paired with crunchy radishes and tender yellow squash, it makes a filling, nutrient-dense side.

½ PLATE

PREP TIME:
15 minutes

COOK TIME:
5 minutes

PER SERVING:
Calories: 82
Total fat: 6g
Saturated fat: 2g
Cholesterol: 4mg
Sodium: 161mg
Carbs: 4g
Fiber: 2g
Sugars: 1g
Protein: 4g

1 bunch broccolini

1 bunch radishes, thinly sliced

1 yellow squash, thinly sliced

½ cup plain 2% Greek yogurt

1 tablespoon whole-grain mustard

1 tablespoon freshly squeezed lemon juice

1 teaspoon extra-virgin olive oil

1 garlic clove, minced

1. Fill a large bowl with ice water and set aside.

2. Fill a large pot with a couple of inches of water and a steaming basket. Bring the water to a boil over high heat. Add the broccolini, cover, and steam until just tender yet still bright green, about 3 minutes. Remove immediately and submerge in the ice bath.

3. Arrange the broccolini on a serving platter and top with the sliced radishes and squash.

4. In a small bowl, whisk together the yogurt, mustard, lemon juice, olive oil, and garlic. Pour the dressing over the vegetables and serve.

Tip: If you don't have access to broccolini, use standard broccoli or Chinese broccoli in its place. Adjust the cook time accordingly to ensure that the broccoli is fork-tender after steaming.

Five-Minute Brussels Sprouts and Almonds

SERVES 4 (½ CUP EACH) I don't always have time to roast Brussels sprouts, so I created this recipe purely as a time-saving way to eat one of my favorite vegetables. If you are looking for a quick, low-carb addition to any meal, this might just become your new go-to. You'll have a flavorful dish, packed with nutrients, ready in minutes.

½ **PLATE**

PREP TIME:
5 minutes

COOK TIME:
7 minutes

PER SERVING:
Calories: 111
Total fat: 8g
Saturated fat: 1g
Cholesterol: 1mg
Sodium: 33mg
Carbs: 7g
Fiber: 3g
Sugars: 2g
Protein: 4g

2 cups Brussels sprouts

¼ cup almonds

1 tablespoon extra-virgin olive oil

2 garlic cloves, minced

¼ teaspoon freshly ground black pepper

¼ cup chopped fresh parsley

1 tablespoon grated Parmesan cheese

Juice of ½ lime

1. Combine the Brussels sprouts and almonds in a food processor. Pulse a few times, until very coarsely chopped.

2. In a large skillet, heat the olive oil over medium-high heat. Add the Brussels sprouts and almonds and cook until the sprouts are slightly browned, 4 to 5 minutes.

3. Stir in the garlic and black pepper and cook for an additional 1 to 2 minutes.

4. Turn off the heat and stir in the parsley. Sprinkle the Parmesan cheese and lime juice over the top. Serve immediately.

Tip: Both almonds and Brussels sprouts are good sources of potassium, so eating this dish is an excellent way to include this important mineral in your diet. Since potassium helps regulate the fluids in our bodies while maintaining normal blood pressure, it's especially helpful for individuals with diabetes, who are at a higher risk of hypertension, also known as high blood pressure.

Braised Turnips and Greens in a Creamy Coconut Sauce

SERVES 4 (½ CUP EACH) Turnips can be eaten along with their greens and, just as with beets, each is a wonderful complement to the other. In this Indian-inspired preparation, creamy coconut milk adds to the dish, combining sweet and savory for a filling and simply prepared side that pairs well with meat and seafood dishes alike.

½ PLATE

PREP TIME:
10 minutes

COOK TIME:
12 minutes

PER SERVING:
Calories: 119
Total fat: 7g
Saturated fat: 3g
Cholesterol: 0mg
Sodium: 416mg
Carbs: 14g
Fiber: 4g
Sugars: 8g
Protein: 2g

1 bunch turnips, with greens

1 tablespoon organic canola oil

½ teaspoon mustard seeds

½ onion, finely chopped

2 tablespoons water

1 teaspoon ground turmeric

½ teaspoon salt

¼ cup coconut milk

1. Remove the turnips from their greens and cut the turnips into 1-inch chunks. Cut the leaves in half lengthwise, stack them in a pile, and then cut them cross-wise into thin strips.

2. In a large skillet, heat the oil over medium-high heat. Add the mustard seeds and cook until they stop popping. Add the onion and sauté until it begins to soften, 2 to 3 minutes.

3. Add the turnips, greens, water, turmeric, and salt. Cover and reduce the heat to medium. Cook until the turnips are tender, 5 to 7 minutes.

4. Remove the lid and return the heat to medium-high. Cook off any excess liquid that remains in the pan. Add the coconut milk and stir until heated through. Serve.

Sautéed Garlic, Ginger, and Shallot Green Beans

½ PLATE

PREP TIME:
10 minutes

COOK TIME:
10 minutes

PER SERVING:
Calories: 71
Total fat: 4g
Saturated fat: 1g
Cholesterol: 0mg
Sodium: 153mg
Carbs: 9g
Fiber: 3g
Sugars: 4g
Protein: 2g

SERVES 4 (⅔ CUP EACH) Brought to life with fresh ginger, shallots, and garlic, these green beans pop with flavor and are a perfect complement to both meat and veggie main dishes. The beans are blanched first to parcook them, then quickly sautéed in the aromatics to maximize flavor.

1 pound green beans, trimmed

1 tablespoon extra-virgin olive oil

1 shallot, minced

2 garlic cloves, minced

2-inch knob ginger, minced

¼ teaspoon salt

1. Fill a large bowl with ice water and set aside.

2. Bring a large pot of salted water to a boil over high heat. Add the beans and return the water to a boil. Cook until just tender but still bright green, about 3 minutes. Use a slotted spoon to transfer the beans to the ice bath. Allow the beans to cool for 3 minutes, then transfer them to a colander to drain. Pat them dry with paper towels or a clean kitchen towel.

3. In a large skillet, heat the oil over medium heat. Add the shallot, garlic, and ginger and sauté until the garlic turns a light golden brown and the shallot becomes tender.

4. Add the green beans to the skillet and toss until heated through, 2 to 3 minutes. Season with the salt and serve.

Grilled Zucchini Salad

SERVES 4 (1 ZUCCHINI EACH) Preparation doesn't have to be complicated to lock in the flavor of summer. This minimalist salad draws on the abundance of zucchini in the summer season and looks lovely on the plate. Make the salad using young zucchini from your garden—or simply buy them year-round from the market.

4 small zucchini

¼ cup extra-virgin olive oil

¼ cup white wine vinegar

1 tablespoon Dijon mustard

½ tablespoon maple syrup

2 garlic cloves, minced

½ teaspoon salt

½ teaspoon freshly ground black pepper

Leaves from 3 fresh mint sprigs, for garnish

½ PLATE

PREP TIME:
10 minutes
+ 2 hours to marinate

COOK TIME:
5 minutes

PER SERVING:
Calories: 166
Total fat: 14g
Saturated fat: 2g
Cholesterol: 0mg
Sodium: 397mg
Carbs: 9g
Fiber: 2g
Sugars: 6g
Protein: 3g

1. Cut the stem end off each zucchini. Cut the zucchini on the bias into thin ovals.

2. In a small bowl, whisk together the olive oil, vinegar, mustard, maple syrup, garlic, salt, and pepper. Pour the marinade over the zucchini. Cover and refrigerate for 2 hours.

3. Preheat a grill to medium-high.

4. Grill the zucchini slices for 1 to 2 minutes on each side, until just tender. Transfer to a serving platter and garnish with the mint.

Creamy Cauliflower and Cheese Bake

SERVES 4 (1 CUP EACH) Any warm, cheesy dish represents the definition of what comfort food is to me. This recipe tastes rich and creamy, yet has been lightened up a bit. It can be served as a side dish or even as a snack between meals. Steaming the cauliflower first ensures that it is tender and prevents the finished dish from being weighed down with extra water from the cauliflower cooking.

½ PLATE

PREP TIME:
10 minutes

COOK TIME:
45 minutes

PER SERVING:
Calories: 183
Total fat: 13g
Saturated fat: 4g
Cholesterol: 13mg
Sodium: 391mg
Carbs: 11g
Fiber: 4g
Sugars: 3g
Protein: 8g

1 medium head cauliflower, broken into small florets

2 tablespoons extra-virgin olive oil

1 tablespoon whole-wheat flour

2 cups unsweetened almond milk

¼ teaspoon ground nutmeg

¼ teaspoon salt

¼ teaspoon freshly ground black pepper

¼ cup grated Parmesan cheese

¼ cup grated Swiss cheese

1. Preheat the oven to 375°F.

2. Fill a large pot with a couple of inches of water and a steaming basket. Bring the water to a boil over high heat. Add the cauliflower, cover, and steam for 5 minutes. Drain and set aside.

3. In a small saucepan, heat the oil over medium-high heat. Add the flour and whisk constantly for 2 minutes.

4. Pour the almond milk slowly into the pan, whisking constantly, until the sauce thickens, about 10 minutes. Remove the pan from the heat and stir in the nutmeg, salt, pepper, Parmesan cheese, and Swiss cheese. ▶

5. Pour half of the sauce into the bottom of a 1½-quart casserole dish. Add the cauliflower, then pour the remaining sauce over the cauliflower.

6. Bake until the sauce is bubbly and the top of the casserole is beginning to brown, about 25 minutes.

Tip: If you prefer, you can use frozen cauliflower in place of fresh. Put the frozen cauliflower in a colander and let it thaw and drain for 30 minutes, then shake out the excess water.

Roasted Beets and Greens with Balsamic Dressing

SERVES 4 (2 CUPS EACH) Beets are subtly sweet, but this is no reason to avoid them altogether. Loaded with vitamins and minerals, beets contain a good deal of fiber, making them a great addition to your diabetes eating plan. This recipe uses both the beetroot and the greens, creating a complexly flavored side dish that works well with both meat and vegetable mains.

½ PLATE

PREP TIME:
10 minutes

COOK TIME:
1 hour 10 minutes

PER SERVING:
Calories: 127
Total fat: 9g
Saturated fat: 2g
Cholesterol: 8mg
Sodium: 153mg
Carbs: 10g
Fiber: 2g
Sugars: 7g
Protein: 3g

2 bunches beets, with greens attached

2 tablespoons extra-virgin olive oil

¼ cup chopped red onion

2 garlic cloves, minced

¼ cup balsamic vinegar

¼ cup crumbed feta cheese

1. Remove the beets from the greens, leaving about 1 inch of stem on each beet. Scrub the beets under running water.

2. Fill a large pot with a couple of inches of water and a steaming basket. Bring the water to a boil over high heat. Add the beets, cover, and steam until the beets are tender when pierced with a fork, 45 to 60 minutes. Drain and set aside.

3. Rinse the beet greens, then remove the stalks from the leaves and discard. Cut the leaves into bite-size pieces. Dry the leaves with a clean kitchen towel, salad spinner, or paper towels.

4. In a skillet, heat the olive oil over medium heat. Add the onion and sauté until softened, 3 to 4 minutes. Add the garlic and the beet greens and toss to coat. Cover, reduce the heat to medium-low, and cook until the greens are wilted, 3 to 4 minutes.

5. Trim the roots from the cooled beets and slip off their skins. Cut the beets into ¼-inch-thick rounds and arrange them on a serving plate. Top the beet rounds with the beet green mixture, drizzle with the balsamic vinegar, and top with the feta cheese.

Sweet Potato Fries

Starch and Grain Sides

When most people think of comfort food, they probably imagine warm starches like potatoes, rice, and mac and cheese. While I've never met a person who didn't enjoy these foods, we all realize they aren't exactly the key to better health and blood sugar management. However, this doesn't mean we need to omit them completely from our diets. We all need to indulge in our warm starches and grains when we want them; in fact, they can actually provide powerful nutritional benefits!

For this chapter, I gathered all the most nutritious starches and grains to create new and improved adaptations of their traditional comfort food versions. Though these recipes still taste like the classics we know and love, I have amplified their nutrient content to produce dishes you will never need to think twice about enjoying again.

Crispy Sage-Roasted Root Vegetables

SERVES 4 (½ CUP EACH) If you are looking for a new way to love eating your vegetables, this is it! With four different root vegetables, this recipe will give you a new appreciation for the incredible taste variety vegetables can provide.

1 medium sweet potato, peeled and diced

2 new potatoes, diced

2 beets, diced

3 carrots, peeled and cut into 1-inch pieces

1 tablespoon extra-virgin olive oil

15 fresh sage leaves

1 teaspoon garlic powder

1. Preheat the oven to 400°F. Line a baking sheet with parchment paper.

2. Toss together all the ingredients on the lined baking sheet. Roast, tossing once halfway through, until the sweet potatoes are slightly browned and the beets are soft inside, 25 to 35 minutes. Remove the sage leaves prior to serving.

¼ **PLATE**

PREP TIME:
5 minutes

COOK TIME:
35 minutes

PER SERVING:
Calories: 110
Total fat: 4g
Saturated fat: 1g
Cholesterol: 0mg
Sodium: 85mg
Carbs: 19g
Fiber: 4g
Sugar: 7g
Protein: 2g

Old-Fashioned Sweet Potato Bake with Pecans

¼ PLATE

PREP TIME:
10 minutes

COOK TIME:
1 hour 15 minutes

PER SERVING:
Calories: 97
Total fat: 4g
Saturated fat: 1g
Cholesterol: 52mg
Sodium: 41mg
Carbs: 13g
Fiber: 2g
Sugars: 4g
Protein: 3g

SERVES 8 (½ CUP EACH) To me, sweet potatoes are the ultimate comfort food. Growing up in the South, I remember every celebration including some form of sweet potato dish. This one is my mom's original recipe. There is just something magical about the combination of warm sweet potatoes and local pecans. Though I can't quite explain it, I think you'll understand when you take a bite!

Nonstick cooking spray

2 pounds sweet potatoes (about 4 medium potatoes)

½ teaspoon ground cinnamon

2 tablespoons freshly squeezed orange juice

2 large eggs

¼ cup chopped pecans

1. Preheat the oven to 350°F. Lightly coat an 8-inch square baking dish with nonstick cooking spray.

2. Fill a large pot with water and bring to a boil over high heat. Add the sweet potatoes, reduce the heat, and slow-boil the potatoes until a fork can be inserted in each potato easily, about 30 minutes. Drain the potatoes and cool. Peel the potatoes.

3. Transfer the potatoes to the bowl of an electric mixer and lightly beat them. Add the cinnamon, orange juice, and eggs. Whip on high until all the ingredients are incorporated and the mixture is slightly fluffy, about 45 seconds.

4. Pour the mixture into the prepared baking dish. Bake for 40 minutes. Sprinkle the pecans evenly across the top and bake for another 5 minutes.

Tip: While sweet potatoes are considered a starchy vegetable, they are lower on the glycemic index than white potatoes. They are also much higher in vitamin A, a key vitamin that promotes normal vision, regulates our immune system, and protects us from infections.

Sweet Potato Fries

SERVES 4 (1 POTATO EACH) Baked rather than fried, these sweet potato fries are crisp like a French fry but in a league of their own in terms of flavor. As their name rightly indicates, they have an impressive sweetness that blends wonderfully with cinnamon. Cinnamon is a strategic spice in this recipe, since research suggests a possible benefit to blood sugar.

4 medium sweet potatoes

1 tablespoon extra-virgin olive oil

1 teaspoon ground cinnamon

¼ teaspoon salt

¼ teaspoon cayenne pepper (optional)

1. Preheat the oven to 425°F.

2. Cut the sweet potatoes lengthwise into disks, then stack the disks into piles and cut the disks into strips.

3. In a large bowl, toss the sweet potatoes with the olive oil until lightly coated. Add the cinnamon, salt, and cayenne pepper (if using) and toss again.

4. Arrange the potatoes in a single layer on a dark baking sheet. Bake, flipping once about halfway through cooking, until crisp and browned, 30 to 40 minutes. Serve hot.

¼ PLATE

PREP TIME:
10 minutes

COOK TIME:
40 minutes

PER SERVING:
Calories: 134
Total fat: 4g
Saturated fat: 1g
Cholesterol: 0mg
Sodium: 187mg
Carbs: 24g
Fiber: 4g
Sugars: 7g
Protein: 2g

Mediterranean Oven-Roasted Potatoes and Vegetables with Herbs

¼ PLATE

PREP TIME:
10 minutes

COOK TIME:
25 minutes

PER SERVING:
Calories: 108
Total fat: 5g
Saturated fat: 1g
Cholesterol: 0mg
Sodium: 209mg
Carbs: 14g
Fiber: 3g
Sugars: 4g
Protein: 3g

SERVES 6 (1 CUP EACH) Warm roasted vegetables are always part of my weekly meal plan. This Mediterranean version contains a variety of vegetables with savory, fresh herbs. Herbs are one of the best ways to season food since they are sodium free, while adding flavor and antioxidants to our meal.

8 ounces fingerling potatoes, quartered

8 ounces miniature red bell peppers, halved lengthwise and seeded

8 ounces mushrooms, sliced

1 cup cauliflower florets

1 onion, sliced

2 tablespoons extra-virgin olive oil

½ teaspoon salt

½ teaspoon freshly ground black pepper

1 tablespoon chopped fresh rosemary

1 tablespoon chopped fresh oregano

1 tablespoon chopped fresh parsley

1. Preheat the oven to 425ºF.

2. In a large bowl, combine the potatoes, peppers, mushrooms, cauliflower, and onion. Drizzle with the olive oil, salt, and pepper and toss to combine.

3. Arrange the vegetables in a single layer on a baking sheet. Bake for 25 minutes, stirring once. Remove from the oven and toss with the rosemary, oregano, and parsley. Serve.

Mashed Cauliflower and Potatoes

¼ PLATE

PREP TIME:
10 minutes

COOK TIME:
10 minutes

PER SERVING:
Calories: 125
Total fat: 3g
Saturated fat: 1g
Cholesterol: 5mg
Sodium: 247mg
Carbs: 23g
Fiber: 4g
Sugars: 4g
Protein: 4g

SERVES 6 (½ CUP EACH) This healthier remake of classic mashed potatoes combines the mildly flavored cauliflower with potatoes for a lower-carb version of the old favorite. Leaving the skins on adds more fiber and flavor. Pair mashed potatoes with a lean protein and another nonstarchy vegetable such as the Simple Green Salad with Garlic, Lemon, and Olive Oil Vinaigrette (page 145) to make your meal balanced.

1 pound new potatoes, cut into 1-inch cubes

1 large head cauliflower

¼ cup unsweetened almond milk

1 tablespoon unsalted butter

½ teaspoon salt

¼ teaspoon freshly ground black pepper

2 tablespoons chopped fresh chives

1. Put the potatoes in a large pot. Cover with water and bring to a boil over medium-high heat. Cook until the potatoes are tender when pierced with a fork, about 10 minutes. Drain and return to the pot.

2. Meanwhile, fill another large pot with a couple of inches of water and a steaming basket. Bring the water to a boil over high heat. Add the cauliflower, cover, and steam until tender, 6 to 8 minutes. Drain and add to the pot with the potatoes.

3. Using a potato masher, mash the potatoes and cauliflower together to the desired consistency. Add the almond milk, butter, salt, pepper, and chives and mix well. Serve hot.

Black-Eyed Peas and Kale Salad

SERVES 8 (½ CUP EACH) This filling salad stands out for its uncomplicated preparation and minimal ingredients. While black-eyed peas are traditionally known as a New Year's Day food, their creamy texture and malleable flavor make them a great choice for everyday eating. This is a hearty vegetable side that pairs well with lighter main dishes.

1 pound dried black-eyed peas, soaked in water overnight

1 bunch kale, stemmed, leaves cut into bite-size pieces

3 tablespoons extra-virgin olive oil

10 garlic cloves, minced

1 teaspoon salt

1. In a large pot, cover the beans with a couple of inches of water and bring to a boil over high heat. Reduce the heat and simmer until the beans are tender, 40 to 50 minutes. Drain and transfer to a large bowl.

2. Fill the same large pot with water and bring to a boil over high heat. Add the kale and cook until the kale is tender yet still bright green, 2 to 3 minutes.

3. Remove the kale with a slotted spoon and transfer it to the bowl with the beans.

4. Add the olive oil, garlic, and salt and mix well. Serve hot or cold.

Tip: Black-eyed peas are not commonly sold canned like many other beans, making it necessary to cook them from their dried state. Cooking dried beans allows you more control over your sodium intake, as canned beans often contain added salt. When you see how easy the process is in this recipe, you may want to start cooking other dried beans as well and ditching canned altogether.

¼ PLATE

PREP TIME:
10 minutes

COOK TIME:
1 hour

PER SERVING:
Calories: 251
Total fat: 6g
Saturated fat: 1g
Cholesterol: 0mg
Sodium: 310mg
Carbs: 37g
Fiber: 7g
Sugars: 4g
Protein: 14g

Wheat Berry and Tabbouleh Salad

SERVES 6 (¾ CUP EACH) Vegetables are the stars of this filling salad that plays on classic Middle Eastern flavors. Using the wheat berry, the whole-grain form of the plant used to make flour, this salad can be eaten on its own, or rolled up in a lettuce wrap with an additional source of protein for an easy meal. Be sure to use fresh herbs and lemon juice, as their bright flavors are some of the biggest contributors to this salad.

¼ PLATE

PREP TIME:
10 minutes

COOK TIME:
1 hour

PER SERVING:
Calories: 172
Total fat: 7g
Saturated fat: 1g
Cholesterol: 0mg
Sodium: 103mg
Carbs: 24g
Fiber: 5g
Sugars: 1g
Protein: 5g

1 cup wheat berries

3 cups water

1 cup chopped tomato

1 cup chopped cucumber

¼ cup sliced scallions

½ cup chopped fresh parsley

1 tablespoon chopped fresh mint

3 tablespoons extra-virgin olive oil

3 tablespoons freshly squeezed lemon juice

¼ teaspoon salt

1. In a small pot, combine the wheat berries and water. Bring to a boil over high heat, then reduce the heat to a simmer. Cover and cook until tender, 45 to 60 minutes.

2. In a large bowl, combine the cooked wheat berries, tomato, cucumber, scallions, parsley, and mint. Toss to combine.

3. In a small bowl, whisk together the olive oil, lemon juice, and salt. Pour over the salad and toss to combine. Serve immediately or chill in the refrigerator until serving time.

eat what you love DIABETES COOKBOOK

Wild Rice Pilaf with Broccoli and Carrots

SERVES 8 (½ CUP EACH) Wild rice boasts a nutty, firm texture that sets it apart from other rice varieties. Typically ebony in appearance, wild rice is actually a separate species, though closely related to other types of rice. Here it is paired with brown rice, broccoli, and carrots for a nutritious, savory side dish that shows off this unique grain at its best.

¼ PLATE

PREP TIME:
10 minutes

COOK TIME:
1 hour 30 minutes

PER SERVING:
Calories: 210
Total fat: 8g
Saturated fat: 1g
Cholesterol: 0mg
Sodium: 340mg
Carbs: 29g
Fiber: 2g
Sugars: 2g
Protein: 6g

Nonstick cooking spray

4 cups low-sodium chicken broth

¾ cup wild rice

¾ cup long-grain brown rice

¼ cup extra-virgin olive oil

1 large onion, chopped

2 carrots, peeled and chopped

½ teaspoon dried thyme

2 garlic cloves, minced

3 cups broccoli florets

1 teaspoon salt

½ teaspoon freshly ground black pepper

1. Preheat the oven to 350°F. Lightly coat a 2-quart casserole dish with nonstick cooking spray.

2. In a large pot, combine the broth, wild rice, and brown rice. Bring to a boil over high heat, then reduce the heat to medium. Cover and cook until the water is absorbed and the rice is tender, about 45 minutes. Let stand for 10 minutes, covered.

3. In a large skillet, heat the olive oil over medium-high heat. Add the onion, carrots, and thyme, and sauté until the onion becomes translucent, 5 to 7 minutes. Add the garlic and sauté for 1 additional minute. Remove the skillet from the heat.

4. Stir in the broccoli, rice, salt, and pepper. Transfer the mixture to the casserole dish, cover, and bake until the broccoli is tender, about 30 minutes.

Quinoa and Vegetable Pilau

SERVES 6 (¾ CUP EACH) Pilau, an Indian dish also called pilaf, is a one-pot dish that delivers. At once spicy and savory, this is a perfect low-fat side to complement heavier meat dishes. Bursting with flavor, this recipe uses a combination of whole spices common in Indian cooking. Be sure to tell guests not to eat these spices or, if you prefer, simply remove them before serving.

1 teaspoon organic canola oil

1 medium onion, sliced

2 garlic cloves, crushed

4 cardamom pods

1 cinnamon stick

2 whole cloves

1 dried red chile

1 leek, thinly sliced on the bias

½ red bell pepper, sliced

½ yellow bell pepper, sliced

1 cup quinoa

2 cups water

1 teaspoon coriander seeds

½ teaspoon salt

1 small zucchini, sliced

¼ PLATE

PREP TIME:
10 minutes

COOK TIME:
30 minutes

PER SERVING:
Calories: 146
Total fat: 3g
Saturated fat: 0g
Cholesterol: 0mg
Sodium: 203mg
Carbs: 26g
Fiber: 4g
Sugars: 2g
Protein: 5g

1. In a large pot, heat the oil over medium-high heat. Add the onion and sauté until it begins to soften, 3 to 4 minutes. Add the garlic and sauté for 1 minute. Add the cardamom pods, cinnamon stick, cloves, and chile and sauté for 1 minute. Add the leek and bell peppers and sauté for 2 minutes.

2. Add the quinoa and water. Bring to a boil and add the coriander seeds and salt. Reduce the heat to low, cover, and simmer for 15 minutes. Add the zucchini, cover, and continue to cook until the quinoa is tender and the liquid has evaporated, about 5 minutes. Fluff with a fork, remove the whole spices if desired, and serve.

Roasted Broccoli and Parmesan Millet Bake

SERVES 8 (1 CUP EACH) Millet, like quinoa, is a gluten-free grain, but it costs about half as much. Millet is easy to cook and works wonderfully in casseroles such as this one, where it combines with savory Parmesan cheese and broccoli for a filling and creamy side dish.

¼ PLATE

PREP TIME:
10 minutes

COOK TIME:
40 minutes

PER SERVING:
Calories: 332
Total fat: 14g
Saturated fat: 6g
Cholesterol: 25mg
Sodium: 561mg
Carbs: 35g
Fiber: 6g
Sugars: 2g
Protein: 18g

8 cups broccoli florets

2 tablespoons extra-virgin olive oil, divided

½ teaspoon freshly ground black pepper

Nonstick cooking spray

1½ cups millet

3 cups water

3 garlic cloves, minced

1 cup unsweetened almond milk

1 teaspoon dried thyme

¾ teaspoon salt, divided

8 ounces grated Parmesan cheese

1. Preheat the oven to 450ºF.

2. In a large mixing bowl, toss the broccoli with 1 tablespoon of olive oil and the pepper. Spread out the broccoli in a single layer on a large baking sheet and roast for 20 minutes, stirring once about halfway through. Remove and set aside.

3. Reduce the oven temperature to 400ºF. Lightly coat a 2-quart casserole dish with nonstick cooking spray.

4. While the broccoli is cooking, in a small pot, combine the millet and water. Bring the water to a boil over high heat, then reduce the heat to a simmer. Cover and cook until all the water is absorbed and the millet is tender, about 15 minutes. Fluff with a fork.

5. In a skillet, heat the remaining 1 tablespoon of olive oil over medium-low heat. Sauté the garlic for 1 minute. Add the almond milk, thyme, and ¼ teaspoon of salt. Add the Parmesan cheese, stirring until it melts. Turn off the heat.

6. Transfer the millet to the casserole dish and toss with the remaining ½ teaspoon of salt. Fold in the broccoli, pour the cheese mixture over the casserole, and stir to combine. Bake the casserole, uncovered, until warmed through, about 15 minutes.

Easy, Cheesy Quinoa Fritters

SERVES 5 (2 FRITTERS EACH) Both kids and adults enjoy these flavorful fritters as either a main dish or a side. Quinoa is considered a complete protein, meaning it contains all nine of the essential amino acids we need for optimal health. These fritters can be made with a variety of vegetables, so feel free to throw in your favorite if it is not already included in the ingredients list below.

1 cup cooked quinoa (prepared with low-sodium chicken broth instead of water)

1 large egg, beaten

¼ cup shredded nonfat mozzarella cheese

¼ cup whole-wheat bread crumbs

¼ cup finely chopped spinach

2 tablespoons finely chopped yellow onion

2 tablespoons finely chopped scallion

3 fresh basil leaves, minced

1 tablespoon garlic powder

¼ teaspoon freshly ground black pepper

⅛ teaspoon salt

1 tablespoon extra-virgin olive oil

1. Combine all the ingredients except the olive oil in a small mixing bowl.

2. Heat the olive oil in a medium skillet over medium-high heat. Once the oil is hot, place heaping spoonfuls of the quinoa mixture into the hot skillet (you may need to work in batches). Cook until lightly browned, 3 to 4 minutes each side. Serve warm.

Tip: Quinoa contains iron, fiber for digestive health, magnesium, and B vitamins to increase your energy and metabolism. While it does contain carbs, quinoa is still a good choice for individuals with diabetes, since its fiber and protein content help manage blood sugar levels, as opposed to other refined starches.

¼ PLATE

PREP TIME:
10 minutes

COOK TIME:
10 minutes

PER SERVING:
Calories: 142
Total fat: 6g
Saturated fat: 2g
Cholesterol: 45mg
Sodium: 138mg
Carbs: 15g
Fiber: 2g
Sugars: 1g
Protein: 7g

Macaroni and Cheese with Mixed Vegetables

SERVES 8 (¾ CUP EACH) Macaroni and cheese is a comfort-food classic, and with this reworking, it can be part of your regular eating plan as well. Loading the dish with broccoli and cauliflower lowers the carb count while still allowing you to savor that distinctive gooey, rich, cheesy goodness.

¼ PLATE

PREP TIME:
10 minutes

COOK TIME:
1 hour

PER SERVING:
Calories: 176
Total fat: 7g
Saturated fat: 3g
Cholesterol: 67mg
Sodium: 326mg
Carbs: 20g
Fiber: 4g
Sugars: 1g
Protein: 11g

Nonstick cooking spray

1½ cups whole-wheat elbow noodles

4 cups frozen broccoli and cauliflower mix, thawed in a colander

1 cup shredded sharp Cheddar cheese, divided

2 large eggs, beaten

2 cups unsweetened almond milk

1 teaspoon onion powder

½ teaspoon mustard powder

½ teaspoon salt

½ teaspoon freshly ground black pepper

1. Preheat the oven to 350°F. Coat a 9-inch square baking dish with nonstick cooking spray.

2. Bring a large pot of water to a boil over high heat. Cook the noodles according to the package directions until just tender. Drain.

3. Squeeze any excess moisture from the cauliflower and broccoli and transfer them to the baking dish. Add the noodles and toss with the vegetables. Add ¾ cup of cheese and toss to combine.

4. In a small bowl, whisk together the eggs, almond milk, onion powder, mustard powder, salt, and pepper. Pour this mixture over the noodles and vegetables evenly, and top with the remaining ¼ cup of cheese.

5. Cover with aluminum foil and bake for 40 minutes. Uncover and bake until the top is browned, another 5 to 10 minutes. Let rest for 10 minutes before serving.

Tip: If you prefer to use fresh broccoli and cauliflower instead of frozen, that's fine, too. However, to ensure it is fully cooked and does not leave the mac and cheese watery, steam the vegetables for 5 minutes before mixing with the noodles in step 3.

eat what you love DIABETES COOKBOOK

Broccoli, Chard, and Cheddar Bread Pudding

SERVES 6 (½ CUP EACH) Bread pudding may have sweet roots, but that's no reason it can't be a savory side as well. Combining bits of bread and cheese along with a medley of broccoli, onions, and chard makes a filling and nutritious accompaniment on the table. As the dish cooks, the flavors blend together, and the exposed bread becomes crisp and toasty—perfect elements in a comfort-food side dish

¼ PLATE

PREP TIME:
10 minutes
COOK TIME:
1 hour 10 minutes

PER SERVING:
Calories: 290
Total fat: 17g
Saturated fat: 8g
Cholesterol: 134mg
Sodium: 721mg
Carbs: 21g
Fiber: 6g
Sugars: 4g
Protein: 17g

Nonstick cooking spray

1½ tablespoons extra-virgin olive oil

1 large onion, chopped

2 bunches Swiss chard, stemmed and leaves chopped

3 large eggs, beaten

1¼ cups unsweetened almond milk

2 tablespoons Dijon or whole-grain mustard

2 teaspoons dried sage

1 teaspoon ground nutmeg

¼ teaspoon freshly ground black pepper

5 cups chopped broccoli florets

3 slices whole-grain bread, cut into ½-inch cubes

6 ounces Cheddar cheese, cut into ½-inch cubes

1. Preheat the oven to 375ºF. Lightly coat an 8-by 11-inch baking dish with non-stick cooking spray.

2. In a large skillet, heat the olive oil over medium-high heat Add the onion and sauté until softened, about 5 minutes. Add the chard and sauté until wilted and softened. Set aside.

3. In a small bowl, whisk together the eggs, almond milk, mustard, sage, nutmeg, and pepper.

4. In a large bowl, toss together the broccoli, bread, and cheese. Transfer half of this mixture to the prepared baking dish. Top with the chard. Add the remaining broccoli mixture to the dish. Pour the egg mixture over the top of the casserole, making sure to wet all the bread pieces.

5. Bake for 1 hour, rotating the dish about halfway through. Let rest for 10 minutes before serving.

Chocolate Walnut Brownies

Desserts

Enjoying dessert when you have diabetes is not only possible, it's important! In my experience, I have found that when we eat the foods we love, with just a few healthy adjustments, and in the right portion sizes, we are more likely to stay on track and meet our health goals.

The recipes you will find here show you how to satisfy your sweet tooth without overindulging. They contain natural sources of sweeteners, for example, rather than refined, processed, or artificial sugars. While we don't need to eat dessert on a daily basis, these recipes will give you some go-to options for every situation—whether you just feel like whipping up a single-serving treat for yourself or are searching for an impressive dessert to bring to a party.

My hope is that these recipes will help you realize that an occasional dessert can and should be part of your lifestyle. Take the time to slow down and enjoy every bite!

Creamy Lemon Mousse

SERVES 4 (½ CUP EACH) The creamy texture of this mousse is the definition of comforting, yet it's surprisingly healthy! The avocado provides the nourishing fats that our bodies digest more slowly, giving us the satisfaction we look for in crave-worthy desserts. When I prepare this easy-to-make treat for dinner guests, I love to serve it in stemless wine glasses or crème brûlée dishes to give it a fancy flair.

PREP TIME:
10 minutes +
1 hour to chill

PER SERVING:
Calories: 286
Total fat: 20g
Saturated fat: 6g
Cholesterol: 0mg
Sodium: 33mg
Carbs: 31g
Fiber: 10g
Sugars: 16g
Protein: 3g

2 avocados, pitted and peeled

1 teaspoon freshly grated lemon zest

½ cup freshly squeezed lemon juice

½ cup unsweetened almond milk

½ medium banana

3 dates, soaked overnight and pitted

2 tablespoons unsweetened coconut flakes

4 strawberries, sliced, for garnish

1. Scoop the avocado flesh into a blender. Add the lemon zest and juice, almond milk, banana, and dates and blend until creamy. Refrigerate for 1 hour.

2. Divide among four glasses or bowls and top each portion with coconut flakes and strawberry garnish.

Lemon Tofu Pudding with Mixed Berry Sauce

PREP TIME:
15 minutes +
2 hours to chill

PER SERVING:
Calories: 154
Total fat: 3g
Saturated fat: 0g
Cholesterol: 4mg
Sodium: 32mg
Carbs: 21g
Fiber: 5g
Sugars: 14g
Protein: 13g

SERVES 4 (½ CUP EACH) The amazing thing about tofu is its likeness to a blank canvas, taking on the flavors of whatever ingredients you mix into it. In this quick pudding recipe, soft tofu is blended with Greek yogurt, maple syrup, and a hearty jolt of fresh lemon zest and juice. The result: a smooth and creamy, slightly savory pudding that comes to life when topped with mixed berry sauce, producing a light, bright, protein-rich dessert.

1 pint mixed berries (strawberries, raspberries, blueberries)

½ (12-ounce) package soft tofu

1¼ cups plain nonfat Greek yogurt

2 tablespoons pure maple syrup

2 lemons

1. In a small bowl, mash the berries. Set aside.

2. Combine the tofu, yogurt, and maple syrup in a food processor. Process until smooth.

3. Zest 1 lemon and add the zest to the tofu mixture. Juice both lemons and add the juice. Process again to combine.

4. Transfer the pudding to four cups or bowls. Top each serving with some of the mashed berries. Refrigerate for 2 hours before serving.

Tip: Make these pudding cups up to 1 day in advance, and cover with plastic wrap until ready to serve. Top each cup with the berries just before serving.

Oatmeal Chocolate Chip Cookies

SERVES 18 (1 COOKIE EACH) This healthier version of the traditional chocolate chip cookie adds oatmeal for a little extra fiber and substitutes applesauce for much of the fat to make a lower-calorie cookie. This does not mean these cookies miss the mark on flavor. With all the same crisp gooeyness of your favorite cookies, they are exactly what you need to satisfy your sweet tooth.

1 cup rolled oats

¾ cup whole-wheat flour

¾ teaspoon baking soda

⅓ cup brown sugar

⅔ cup unsweetened applesauce

½ cup plain 2% Greek yogurt

1 large egg

2 tablespoons organic canola oil

1 teaspoon pure vanilla extract

½ cup dark chocolate chips

PREP TIME:
10 minutes

COOK TIME:
10 minutes

PER SERVING:
Calories: 118
Total fat: 6g
Saturated fat: 2g
Cholesterol: 13mg
Sodium: 65mg
Carbs: 15g
Fiber: 2g
Sugars: 7g
Protein: 3g

1. Preheat the oven to 350°F.

2. In a mixing bowl, combine the rolled oats, flour, baking soda, and brown sugar. Stir to combine.

3. In a small bowl, whisk together the applesauce, yogurt, egg, oil, and vanilla. Stir to mix. Transfer the wet ingredients to the dry ingredients and stir to mix well. Fold in the chocolate chips.

4. Drop rounded teaspoons of cookie dough onto a baking sheet, spacing them 2 inches apart. Bake until browned, 9 to 11 minutes. Let the cookies cool for 2 to 3 minutes on the cookie sheet, then transfer them to a wire rack to cool completely. Store in the refrigerator for up to 5 days.

Chocolate Pudding with Berries

PREP TIME:
5 minutes

PER SERVING:
Calories: 81
Total fat: 3g
Saturated fat: 1g
Cholesterol: 0mg
Sodium: 6mg
Carbs: 11g
Fiber: 3g
Sugars: 6g
Protein: 5g

SERVES 4 (½ CUP EACH) Dark chocolate has never tasted so good. Made with just five ingredients, this quick pudding can be eaten right away or refrigerated for a firmer texture. Topped with fresh berries, this is one timeless combination that is easy to make and, with the inclusion of tofu, is packed with protein to keep you satisfied.

1 (12-ounce) package soft tofu

¼ cup unsweetened cocoa powder

1 tablespoon pure maple syrup

¼ cup fresh raspberries

¼ cup fresh blueberries

In a blender, combine the tofu, cocoa power, and maple syrup and process until smooth. Divide the pudding among four cups or bowls and top each serving with some raspberries and blueberries.

eat what you love DIABETES COOKBOOK

Peanut Butter Bites

PREP TIME:
10 minutes +
30 minutes to chill

PER SERVING:
Calories: 45
Total fat: 3g
Saturated fat: 1g
Cholesterol: 0mg
Sodium: 1mg
Carbs: 5g
Fiber: 1g
Sugars: 4g
Protein: 2g

SERVES 12 (1 BALL EACH) Having these dessert bites on hand at all times is one of the best strategies for keeping your indulgences on track. Their sweetness satisfies cravings, and the peanut butter provides real nourishment—all while including less than 50 calories and only 5 grams of carbs overall. I recommend keeping a few in your freezer for a quick treat any time you are in the mood.

¼ cup natural unsalted peanut butter

2 dates, soaked, pitted, and skinned

¼ medium banana

1 teaspoon unsweetened cocoa powder

2 tablespoons unsweetened coconut flakes (optional)

1. Combine the peanut butter, dates, and banana in a food processor and blend until smooth.

2. Put the cocoa powder on a plate. Using a tablespoon, scoop out the peanut butter mixture and roll into balls, then roll each ball in cocoa powder. Place the balls in a container and refrigerate for at least 30 minutes.

3. Prior to serving, sprinkle with coconut flakes (if using).

Tip: Dates' natural sweetness provides a better option than refined or artificial sweeteners. Soaking them overnight allows them to soften and makes them easier to blend.

Chocolate Walnut Brownies

SERVES 12 (1 BROWNIE EACH) If you are wondering whether a brownie recipe that contains dates and chickpeas tastes like dates and chickpeas, the answer is no—it tastes like brownies! This simple whole-food recipe is delicious and mimics the flavor and consistency of the real thing without using any processed sugar or flour. For the best chocolate flavor, use Dutch-process cocoa powder.

PREP TIME:
10 minutes

COOK TIME:
30 minutes

PER SERVING:
Calories: 187
Total fat: 12g
Saturated fat: 5g
Cholesterol: 17mg
Sodium: 86mg
Carbs: 18g
Fiber: 4g
Sugars: 11g
Protein: 4g

Nonstick cooking spray

6 ounces pitted Medjool dates

¼ cup unsweetened almond milk

¼ cup coconut oil, melted

2 teaspoons pure vanilla extract

1 large egg

1 (15-ounce) can chickpeas, rinsed and drained

⅓ cup unsweetened cocoa powder

1 teaspoon baking powder

1 cup walnut pieces

1. Preheat the oven to 350°F. Lightly coat a 9-inch square baking dish with nonstick cooking spray.

2. In a food processor or blender, combine the dates, almond milk, coconut oil, vanilla, egg, chickpeas, cocoa powder, and baking powder. Process until smooth, then fold in the walnuts. Pour the batter into the pan.

3. Bake until a knife inserted in the center comes out clean, 25 to 30 minutes. Let cool for at least 20 minutes before serving.

Tip: Medjool dates are a soft variety of dates that are sun-dried on the tree and then steamed to re-plump after picking. Regarded as one of the best-tasting date varieties, they have become more popular in the American kitchen in the last decade. These sweet fruits are widely available at grocery stores, health food stores, and online.

Blueberry-Almond Galette

SERVES 8 (1 SLICE EACH) If you love the idea of a pie without all the work, a galette is your solution! Using a single pie crust, this rustic treat cuts out the fuss of a traditional fruit pie. Crisp and flaky, the oil crust is made with whole-wheat flour and oats, making it whole grain and fiber-rich. Almonds finish the galette with a little added crunch.

PREP TIME:
20 minutes

COOK TIME:
30 minutes

PER SERVING:
Calories: 182
Total fat: 9g
Saturated fat: 1g
Cholesterol: 0mg
Sodium: 220mg
Carbs: 25g
Fiber: 3g
Sugars: 12g
Protein: 3g

FOR THE CRUST

¼ cup quick oats

¾ cup whole-wheat flour

½ teaspoon salt

¼ cup organic canola oil

3 to 5 tablespoons ice water

Nonstick cooking spray

FOR THE GALETTE

3 cups fresh blueberries

¼ cup pure maple syrup

1 tablespoon freshly squeezed lemon juice

¼ teaspoon salt

1 tablespoon freshly grated lemon zest

¼ cup sliced almonds

TO MAKE THE CRUST

1. In the bowl of a food processor, combine the oats, flour, and salt. Turn on the food processor and drizzle in the oil as the ingredients are mixing. Add 3 table-spoons of ice water and continue processing. Add up to 2 tablespoons more water, 1 tablespoon at a time, until a ball forms and holds together.

2. Transfer the dough to a sheet of waxed paper. Place another sheet of waxed paper on top of the dough and use your palms to flatten the dough. Roll out the dough between the two sheets of waxed paper into a 12-inch circle.

3. Line a large baking sheet with foil and coat the foil with nonstick cooking spray. Remove the waxed paper and transfer the dough circle to the baking sheet.

eat what you DIABETES COOKBOOK

TO MAKE THE GALETTE

1. Preheat the oven to 425ºF.

2. In a small pot, crush the blueberries using a potato masher. Add the maple syrup, lemon juice, and salt. Bring the mixture to a simmer over medium heat, stirring frequently. Cook until slightly reduced, about 10 minutes.

3. Transfer the mixture to the center of the pastry dough, leaving a 2-inch border around the edges. Working quickly, fold the edges of the dough toward the middle of the galette and crimp the edges. Sprinkle the top with the lemon zest and sliced almonds.

4. Bake until the pastry is browned and the blueberry mixture is bubbling, 25 to 30 minutes. Let the galette cool for 15 minutes before serving.

Tip: The dough can be made up to a day in advance. Once mixed, wrap the dough in plastic wrap and flatten it into a disk. When ready to use, place the disk on the counter for 10 minutes before rolling it out.

Cherry Cobbler

SERVES 8 (1 PIECE EACH) Almond flour creates a crumbly, delicious crust that is low in carbs yet still mouthwateringly delicious. Canned cherries are available year-round, making this an accessible dish even if you are not making it during the short cherry season. But if you can get your hands on fresh cherries, substitute 3 cups of pitted fresh cherries for the canned.

PREP TIME:
10 minutes

COOK TIME:
15 minutes

PER SERVING:
Calories: 183
Total fat: 12g
Saturated fat: 4g
Cholesterol: 52mg
Sodium: 66mg
Carbs: 17g
Fiber: 3g
Sugars: 14g
Protein: 5g

Nonstick cooking spray

2 (16-ounce) cans water-packed cherries, drained

3 tablespoons honey, divided

2 tablespoons freshly squeezed lemon juice

½ teaspoon ground cinnamon

1 cup almond flour

1 teaspoon baking powder

2 tablespoons coconut oil, melted

2 large eggs

1. Preheat the oven to 425°F. Coat a cast-iron skillet or 9-inch square baking pan with nonstick cooking spray.

2. In a small bowl, toss together the cherries, 2 tablespoons of honey, lemon juice, and cinnamon. Pour into the prepared skillet or baking pan.

3. In another bowl, combine the almond flour and baking powder. Add the remaining 1 tablespoon of honey, the coconut oil, and the eggs. Mix well. Spoon the mixture evenly over the cherries.

4. Bake for 15 minutes, until the crust is browned. Serve warm

Maple Pumpkin Pie Bites

SERVES 16 (1 BITE EACH) Pumpkin pie is the ultimate Thanksgiving comfort-food favorite, and with this healthier remake, it is a perfect treat any time of the year! Made with navy beans and pumpkin purée, these creamy, crustless bites melt in your mouth and transport you straight to the Thanksgiving holiday.

PREP TIME:
10 minutes

COOK TIME:
45 minutes +
2 hours to chill

PER SERVING:
Calories: 69
Total fat: 1g
Saturated fat: 0g
Cholesterol: 39mg
Sodium: 80mg
Carbs: 12g
Fiber: 1g
Sugars: 7g
Protein: 4g

Nonstick cooking spray

2 cups cooked or canned navy beans, rinsed and drained

1 cup canned 100% pumpkin purée (not pumpkin pie filling)

3 large eggs

½ cup pure maple syrup

1 teaspoon baking powder

1 teaspoon ground cinnamon

½ teaspoon ground ginger

¼ teaspoon ground nutmeg

¼ teaspoon salt

1. Preheat the oven to 350ºF. Coat an 8-inch square baking pan with nonstick cooking spray.

2. In a food processor or blender, combine all the ingredients and process until smooth. Pour the batter into the prepared pan. Bake until lightly browned and a knife inserted in the center comes out clean, about 45 minutes. Let cool a bit, then transfer to the refrigerator to chill for 2 hours before slicing.

eat what you love DIABETES COOKBOOK

Skillet Berry Crisp with Oatmeal Crumbles

SERVES 8 (1 PIECE EACH) Fresh berries are antioxidant powerhouses, so making sure to have plenty in your diet is a must. While their price is higher than other fruits, their antioxidant activity is four times that of most other fruits and ten times that of vegetables. This simple crisp is quick to make, and highlights these delicious fruits to their fullest. Use fresh or frozen fruits to enjoy this simple dessert any time of year.

4 cups fresh or frozen mixed berries (blackberries, raspberries, blueberries)

3 tablespoons honey, divided

½ cup rolled oats

2 tablespoons flaxseed meal

2 tablespoons whole-wheat flour

2 tablespoons organic canola oil

PREP TIME:
10 minutes

COOK TIME:
30 minutes

PER SERVING:
Calories: 122
Total fat: 5g
Saturated fat: 0g
Cholesterol: 0mg
Sodium: 2mg
Carbs: 19g
Fiber: 5g
Sugars: 9g
Protein: 2g

1. Preheat the oven to 350°F.

2. In a mixing bowl, combine the berries and 1 tablespoon of honey. Mix well. Transfer to an 8-inch square baking dish.

3. In a small bowl, combine the rolled oats, flaxseed meal, and flour. In another bowl, mix the canola oil and remaining 2 tablespoons of honey. Mix this into the oat mixture. Using your hands, squeeze together the topping and break it apart into small crumbles over the berries. Continue until the crisp is covered and all the oat mixture is used.

4. Bake until the topping is golden brown and the fruit is bubbly, about 30 minutes. Serve warm.

The Dirty Dozen and Clean Fifteen

A nonprofit and environmental watchdog organization called Environmental Working Group (EWG) looks at data supplied by the U.S. Department of Agriculture (USDA) and the Food and Drug Administration (FDA) about pesticide residues and compiles a list each year of the best and worst pesticide loads found in commercial crops. You can use these lists to decide which fruits and vegetables to buy organic to minimize your exposure to pesticides and which produce is considered safe enough to skip the organics. This does not mean they are pesticide-free, though, so wash these fruits and vegetables thoroughly.

These lists change every year, so make sure you look up the most recent one before you fill your shopping cart. You'll find the most recent lists as well as a guide to pesticides in produce at EWG.org/FoodNews.

THE DIRTY DOZEN

1. Strawberries
2. Apples
3. Nectarines
4. Peaches
5. Celery
6. Grapes
7. Cherries
8. Spinach
9. Tomatoes
10. Sweet bell peppers
11. Cherry Tomatoes
12. Cucumbers

Plus produce contaminated with highly toxic organophosphate insecticides:

+ Hot peppers
+ Kale/collard greens

THE CLEAN FIFTEEN

1. Avocados
2. Sweet Corn
3. Pineapples
4. Cabbage
5. Sweet peas (frozen)
6. Onions
7. Asparagus
8. Mangoes
9. Papayas
10. Kiwi
11. Eggplant
12. Honeydew Melon
13. Grapefruit
14. Cantaloupe
15. Cauliflower

Measurement Conversion Charts

VOLUME EQUIVALENTS (LIQUID)

US STANDARD	US STANDARD (OUNCES)	METRIC (APPROXIMATE)
2 tablespoons	1 fl. oz.	30 mL
¼ cup	2 fl. oz.	60 mL
½ cup	4 fl. oz.	120 mL
1 cup	8 fl. oz.	240 mL
1½ cups	12 fl. oz.	355 mL
2 cups or 1 pint	16 fl. oz.	475 mL
4 cups or 1 quart	32 fl. oz.	1 L
1 gallon	128 fl. oz.	4 L

OVEN TEMPERATURES

FAHRENHEIT (F)	CELSIUS (C) (APPROXIMATE)
250°	120°
300°	150°
325°	165°
350°	180°
375°	190°
400°	200°
425°	220°
450°	230°

VOLUME EQUIVALENTS (DRY)

US STANDARD	METRIC (APPROXIMATE)
⅛ teaspoon	0.5 mL
¼ teaspoon	1 mL
½ teaspoon	2 mL
¾ teaspoon	4 mL
1 teaspoon	5 mL
1 tablespoon	15 mL
¼ cup	59 mL
⅓ cup	79 mL
½ cup	118 mL
⅔ cup	156 mL
¾ cup	177 mL
1 cup	235 mL
2 cups or 1 pint	475 mL
3 cups	700 mL
4 cups or 1 quart	1 L
½ gallon	2 L
1 gallon	4 L

WEIGHT EQUIVALENTS

US STANDARD	METRIC (APPROXIMATE)
½ ounce	15 g
1 ounce	30 g
2 ounces	60 g
4 ounces	115 g
8 ounces	225 g
12 ounces	340 g
16 ounces or 1 pound	455 g

References

Alley, Lynn. *Cooking with Herbs*. Kansas City: Andrews McMeel, 2013.

American Diabetes Association. "Nutrition Therapy Recommendations for the Management of Adults with Diabetes." *Diabetes Care Journal*. October 2013. Accessed August 8, 2016. http://care.diabetesjournals.org/content/diacare/early/2013/10/07/dc13-2042.full.pdf

American Diabetes Association. "Standards of Medical Care in Diabetes—2016." *Diabetes Care Journal*. January 2016. Volume 39, Supplement 1. Accessed August 26, 2016. http://care.diabetesjournals.org/content/suppl/2015/12/21/39.Supplement_1.DC2/2016-Standards-of-Care.pdf

Bauer, Joy. *From Junk Food to Joy Food*. Carlsbad, CA: Hay House, 2016.

Centers for Disease Control and Prevention. *National Diabetes Statistics Report: Estimates of Diabetes and Its Burden in the United States, 2014*. Atlanta, GA: U.S. Department of Health and Human Services, 2014.

Dragonwagon, Crescent. *Dairy Hollow House Soup & Bread Cookbook*. New York: Workman, 1992.

Guo X., Yang B., Tan J., Jiang J., and Li D. "Associations of dietary intakes of anthocyanins and berry fruits with risk of type 2 diabetes mellitus: a systematic review and meta-analysis of prospective cohort studies." *European Journal of Clinical Nutrition* (August 2016) http://www.nature.com/ejcn/journal/vaop/ncurrent/abs/ejcn2016142a.html

Iyer, Raghavan. *660 Curries*. New York: Workman, 2008.

Larson Duyff, R. (2012) *American Dietetic Association Complete Food and Nutrition Guide*. 4th edition. Hoboken, NJ: John Wiley & Sons, Inc.

Robinson, Jo. *Eating on the Wild Side*. New York: Little, Brown, 2013.

Sondhi, Amrita. *The Tastes of Ayurveda*. Vancouver, BC: Arsenal Pulp Press, 2012.

Wood, Rebecca. *The New Whole Foods Encyclopedia*. New York: Penguin, 2010.

Acknowledgments

This book was made possible because of the love and support of so many people. It is the culmination of endless interactions with wonderful clients, patients, and colleagues with whom I've had the pleasure of working over the years.

I'd like to thank the incredible team at Callisto Media, especially my editor, Talia Platz, who made writing this book such an amazing and positive experience. Thank you to Dr. Swe, for her dedication to the field of diabetes and for writing the foreword, for which I am so grateful. And to Dr. Grover and Toby, two professionals with whom I've enjoyed collaborating over the years and have had the pleasure of experiencing your passion for helping others thrive. Thank you both for contributing endorsements. A special thanks to my friend Lisa Cimperman, MS, RD, for her clinical insights and review of the book. I'm so thankful for all of my professional mentors and colleagues who have inspired and empowered me along the way. While there are so many, to name a few: Dr. Barbara Ann Hughes; Kathleen Rigol, MS, RD; Lindsay Stenovec, MS, RD, CEDRD; the ex-newbies and my former co-workers at HealthCare Partners.

I started writing this book when my son was just six months old. So I have to thank him for helping me understand a different level of dedication, time-management, passion, and dream-seeking. And the ultimate thanks to my husband for his unwavering love and support in the process. I'm so thankful for the Lord's blessings in our lives. A special thanks to our "South Bay Crew" of friends, who have helped in numerous ways while I was writing the book; to my fellow new moms, Rose, Erin, and Sara, who understood like no one else how to balance work and motherhood; and to my amazing family. Thank you to my in-laws, Gary and Joyce, the Buehlers, the Olssons, and my brother David and sister-in-law Kelli for simply everything! I'd also like to thank my mom, who taught me how to cook and therefore without her the book wouldn't be possible. Thank you to my dad for always supporting my newest adventure and to both of you for your lifetime of love and encouragement.

Recipe Index

Index

About the Author

Lori Zanini is a Registered Dietitian, Certified Diabetes Educator, and National Media Spokesperson for the Academy of Nutrition and Dietetics, the world's largest organization of food and nutrition professionals. She is the owner of a nutrition consulting business located in Manhattan Beach, California and has over a decade of experience working with individuals with diabetes to manage their diets. Her work has been featured in numerous print and digital publications, including *Women's Health*, *Shape*, *The Chicago Tribune*, and DoctorOz.com. She lives in Los Angeles, California with her husband and son.

About the Foreword Contributor

Dr. Nandar M. Swe is an Endocrinologist currently employed by Davita Health-Care Partners. After graduating from Medical School in Burma (Myanmar), she completed an Internal Medicine Residency at Abington Memorial Hospital in Abington, Pennsylvania, followed by an Endocrinology, Diabetes, and Metabolism Fellowship at Harbor–UCLA/Los Angeles Biomedical Research Institute in Torrance, California. Dr. Swe is Co-Chair of monthly Regional Diabetic Educators' meetings. She strongly believes in educating patients rather than prescribing medications, and emphasizes their active involvement in care plans.